C000230766

A Message from the President of the Republic of Maldives

For a young and developing nation which has only recently become an active member of the family of the world's free nations, a book of this nature is cause for special celebration.

Standing at the crossways of the Indian Ocean, our islands have represented a haven for mariners from time immemorial — a place to repair and reprovision those sailing ships of old and a haven from the tempests, storms, and perils of the deep.

Steadfast in our Islamic faith, Maldivians are a unique fusion of many cultures — an ancient mix of peoples from different parts of the East, out of which has grown a proud and distinctive race.

As this fascinating book demonstrates, the Maldives is rich not only in its wealth of human cultures, but also in its natural maritime treasures.

Together they have helped advance the Maldives to the forefront of the world's free nations.

The beauty of our islands has also contributed greatly to our progress. Our magnificent palm-shrouded islands with their silver beaches and fascinating lagoons have made the Maldives one of the world's most exclusive tourist destinations — a paradise for underwater divers, fishermen, watersports enthusiasts, and those who follow the sun.

Thousands of new friends visit us each year to see and enjoy our unique maritime heritage: one we are determined to preserve for future generations of Maldivians and for the rest of the world.

Tourism and fisheries are the two key areas in my resolve to see that the quality of life for every citizen of the Maldives is improved. These two sectors provide this country with the foreign exchange so vital to the development of permanent infrastructures for social welfare, health services, and universal education. In this respect, our achievements in such a short era of nationhood are cause for pride.

We are young in every respect, not simply as a nation. The majority of Maldivians are under thirty years of age — with all that this implies in terms of human resources and initiative.

Our young population, inheritors of a nation remarkable for its promise, symbolises the determination that has marked our first decades of freedom. Our ancestors have always welcomed foreigners to our shores, making them guests at their homes. The Maldivians of today, as did their forefathers, maintain this tradition of warm and friendly hospitality.

So let me say Welcome. Please feel at home and share with me and my fellow citizens our joy at celebrating freedom, progress, and development.

And enjoy, too, the wonderful islands, people, and marine flora and fauna, here portrayed in this marvellous book, that go to make up the nation of the Maldives.

Maumoon Abdul Gayoom
President of the Republic of Maldives

MALDIVES

Journey through MALDIVES

Mohamed Amin · Duncan Willetts
Peter Marshall

Camerapix Publishers International
NAIROBI

First published 1992 by
Camerapix Publishers International,
P.O. Box 45048,
Nairobi, Kenya

ISBN 1 874041 20 2

This book was designed and produced by
Camerapix Publishers International,
P.O. Box 45048,
Nairobi, Kenya

Edited by Brian Tetley
Production Editor: Debbie Gaiger
Typeset: Kimberly Davis
Design: Craig Dodd

Printed in Hong Kong.

Contents

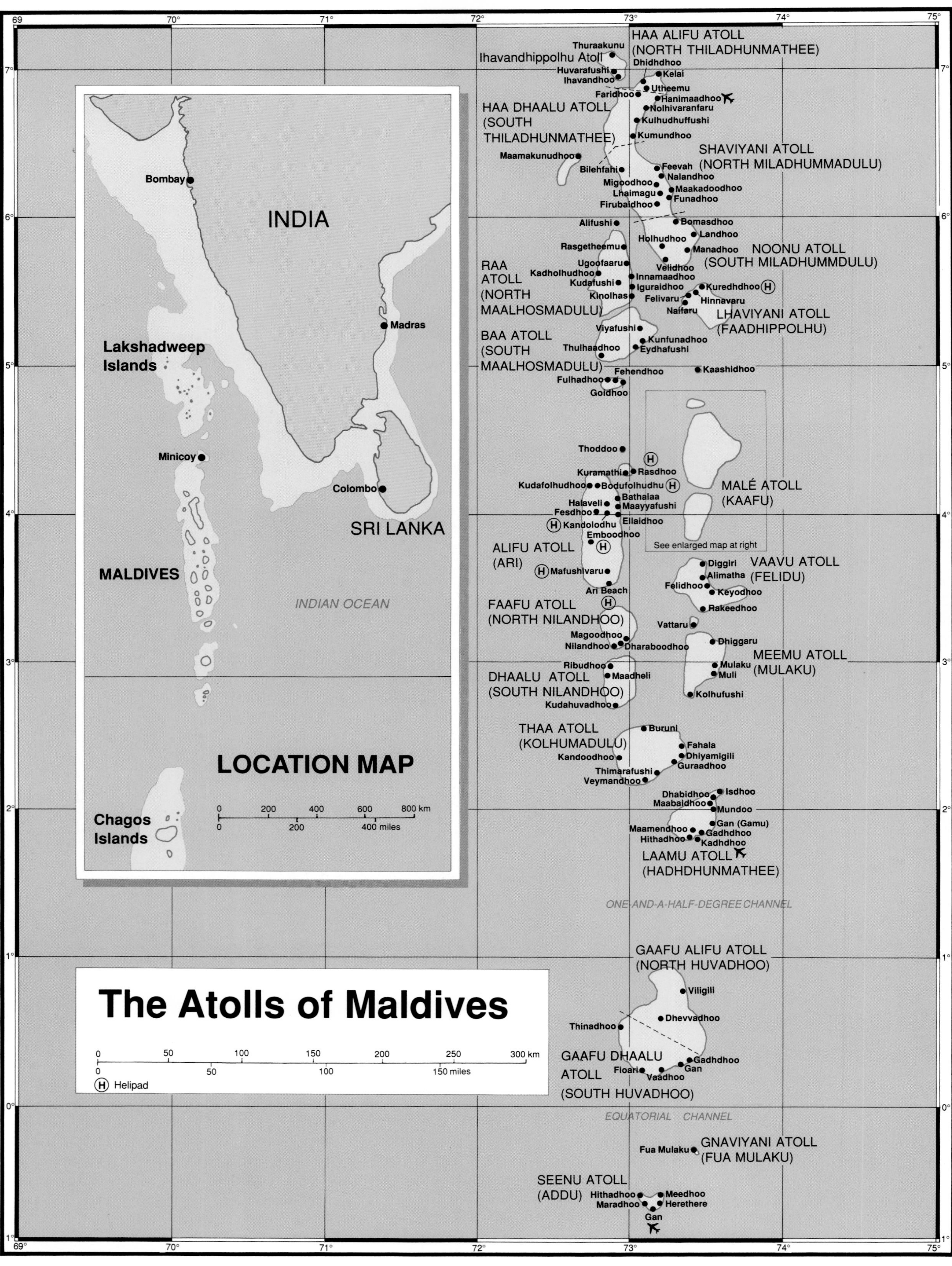

HAA ALIFU ATOLL
(NORTH THILADHUNMATHEE)
Ihavandhippolhu Atoll
HAA DHAALU ATOLL
(SOUTH THILADHUNMATHEE)
SHAVIYANI ATOLL
(NORTH MILADHUMMADULU)
NOONU ATOLL
(SOUTH MILADHUMMDULU)
RAA ATOLL
(NORTH MAALHOSMADULU)
LHAVIYANI ATOLL
(FAADHIPPOLHU)
BAA ATOLL
(SOUTH MAALHOSMADULU)
MALÉ ATOLL
(KAAFU)
See enlarged map at right
ALIFU ATOLL
(ARI)
VAAVU ATOLL
(FELIDU)
FAAFU ATOLL
(NORTH NILANDHOO)
MEEMU ATOLL
(MULAKU)
DHAALU ATOLL
(SOUTH NILANDHOO)
THAA ATOLL
(KOLHUMADULU)
LAAMU ATOLL
(HADHDHUNMATHEE)
ONE-AND-A-HALF-DEGREE CHANNEL
GAAFU ALIFU ATOLL
(NORTH HUVADHOO)
GAAFU DHAALU ATOLL
(SOUTH HUVADHOO)
EQUATORIAL CHANNEL
GNAVIYANI ATOLL
(FUA MULAKU)
SEENU ATOLL
(ADDU)
INDIA
Bombay
Madras
Lakshadweep Islands
Minicoy
Colombo
SRI LANKA
MALDIVES
INDIAN OCEAN
Chagos Islands
LOCATION MAP
0 200 400 600 800 km
0 200 400 miles
The Atolls of Maldives
0 50 100 150 200 250 300 km
0 50 100 150 miles
H Helipad

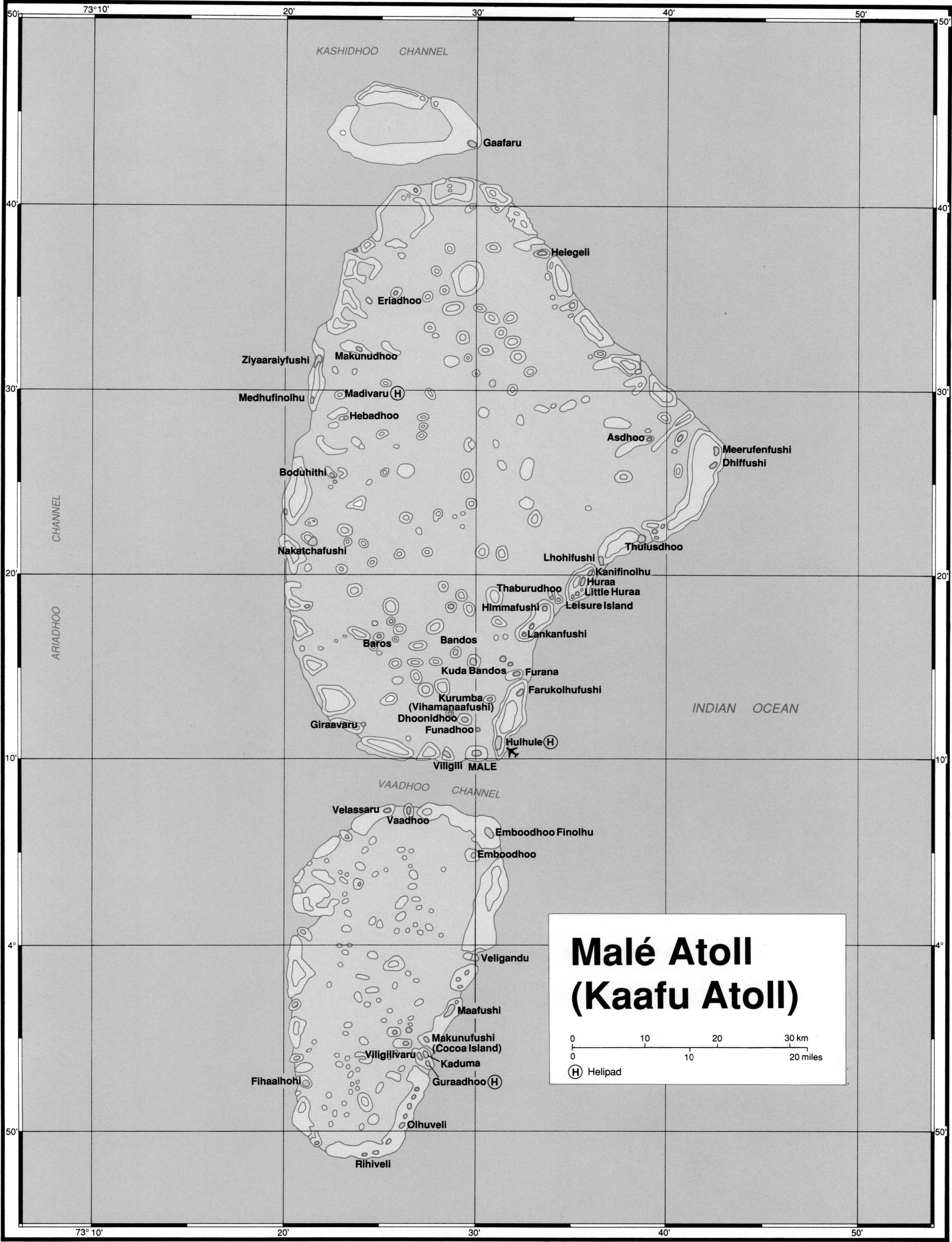

Malé Atoll
(Kaafu Atoll)
0 10 20 30 km
0 10 20 miles
H Helipad
KASHIDHOO CHANNEL
ARIADHOO CHANNEL
VAADHOO CHANNEL
INDIAN OCEAN
Gaafaru
Helegeli
Eriadhoo
Ziyaaraiyfushi
Makunudhoo
Medhufinolhu
Madivaru
Hebadhoo
Asdhoo
Meerufenfushi
Dhiffushi
Boduhithi
Nakatchafushi
Thulusdhoo
Lhohifushi
Kanifinolhu
Huraa
Little Huraa
Thaburudhoo
Himmafushi
Leisure Island
Lankanfushi
Baros
Bandos
Kuda Bandos
Furana
Farukolhufushi
Kurumba
(Vihamanaafushi)
Dhoonidhoo
Funadhoo
Giraavaru
Hulhule
Viligili
MALE
Velassaru
Vaadhoo
Emboodhoo Finolhu
Emboodhoo
Veligandu
Maafushi
Makunufushi
(Cocoa Island)
Viligilivaru
Kaduma
Guraadhoo
Fihaalhohi
Olhuveli
Rihiveli
73°10'
20'
30'
40'
50'

1. Introduction: Journey through Maldives

Maldives is a garland of emerald islands scattered across the Indian Ocean. The lagoons and reefs encircling them make beautiful circular, oblong, and crescent shapes. From the air they look like an ethereal abstract painting. It is as if some artist has splashed jade, turquoise, aquamarine, and azure in subtle disarray on a canvas of darkest blue. You will only find such wondrous shades in the tropics.

Most visitors today fly to Maldives by jumbo jet, but for millenniums the only way to these enchanted isles in the middle of the Indian Ocean was by boat. It is still the best way to arrive. The first thing the seaborne traveller sees on the blue horizon is a green speck that slowly emerges from the sea — an elongated strip soon joined to other similar green strips. As your vessel sails nearer, coconut palms sway in the breeze over the thick foliage; some leaning sharply above the beach in their search for the sun. The long swell curls and crashes over the reef in a savage surge of surf. Beyond the foaming white waters lies the quiet tranquillity of lagoons and pristine coral beaches.

After a gruelling voyage under the tropical sun such sights filled earlier mariners with joy, for the islands meant fresh water, coconuts, and rest — as well as the gracious welcome of a hospitable and gentle people.

Indeed, Maldives has long been celebrated for its rare beauty. That great traveller Marco Polo called it the 'flower of the Indies'. After visiting ninety-two countries, Ibn Battuta declared it the most agreeable place he had ever seen — 'one of the wonders of the world'.

The islands, stretching through the Indian Ocean across the traditional shipping lanes of the region, formed a crucial crossroads for early civilizations. When Cheng Ho travelled from China in the fifteenth century to East Africa he passed through the Maldive islands, as did travellers from Indonesia and the Far East, from the Red Sea and the Persian Gulf. With their beautiful and harmonious blend of Indian, Arabian, African, and Asian features, the faces that greet you when you step ashore in Maldives today reflect this coming and going from time immemorial.

Any navigator wishing to round the southern point of Asia had to travel through the two open channels near the Equator in the southern part of Maldives. In the north the sixty-four-kilometre-wide strait between India and Sri Lanka, filled with reefs, is too shallow for safe passage and the northern Maldive islands form a treacherous barrier.

The double row of atolls that make up the Maldivian archipelago are part of a sharp ridge that rises suddenly out of the ocean. The low-lying islands, surrounded by treacherous reefs and sand bars, are extremely difficult to circumnavigate, especially during the monsoons. As dangerous as a minefield, this maze of islands and reefs has become littered with shipwrecks from all over the world through the centuries.

In Malé Atoll (Kaafu Atoll), Gaafaru Island alone has taken a tremendous toll: in 1873, the 1,174-tonne iron ship *Aracan* sailing from Rangoon to London with general cargo ran aground; in 1879, the s.s. *Sea Gull* was wrecked, as was the 363-tonne barque *Clan Alpine* on her way from Mauritius to Bombay with a cargo of sugar; in 1895, the *Erlangen* was wrecked; and in 1905 the s.s. *Crusader* went down with another cargo of sugar. The most recent victim was the 863-tonne *Lady*

Previous pages: The coral reefs and islands of the Maldivian archipelago stretching across the Equator in the middle of the Indian Ocean were called 'one of the wonders of the world' by the great Arab traveller Ibn Battuta. Islanders call their country Dhivehi Raajje *— Island Kingdom — but ancient seafarers referred to it as* Maladiv, *meaning 'garland of islands'.*

Above: Artefact discovered on Vaadhoo Island in Gaafu Dhaalu Atoll (South Huvadhoo Atoll), one of many among the ruins of remote islands that may belong to the early era of Buddhism or even earlier.

Christine, registered in Panama, which was lost on 16 April 1974.

One of the most famous wrecks was that of the *Corbin* which sank on the western reef of Goidhoo Island between Fulhadhoo and Fehendhoo Islands in Baa Atoll (South Maalhosmadulu Atoll) in 1602. François Pyrard de Laval, who was held captive on the islands for five years, later wrote a wonderful contemporary account of life in Maldives. Another historian who first arrived in 1879 as a shipwrecked castaway was H. C. P. Bell. He was so fascinated by what he found that he returned many times and left some interesting records.

The local term for Maldives is *Dhivehi Raajje*, the 'Island Kingdom'. The inhabitants call themselves *Dhivehin*, meaning islander, and speak their own unique language, *Dhivehi*. Indian traders named the country *Maladiv*, from the Sanskrit for 'garland of islands'. Certainly the country appears like a necklace of emerald gems lying on the blue velvet of the Indian Ocean, and through the Portuguese this name was adopted by other European languages.

Maldives is, in fact, an archipelago of some 1,190 small coral islands, many covered with vegetation, that extends from seven degrees latitude north to south of the Equator. Together with the Lakshadweep (formerly Laccadive) Islands to the north, and the Chagos Islands to the south, they form part of a vast submarine mountain range, on top of which coral reefs have grown. The country consists of a double line of twenty-six natural atolls, 130 kilometres at their widest point, stretching for 823 kilometres. Its nearest neighbours India and Sri Lanka are situated north and east about 600 and 670 kilometres respectively.

Every atoll (the English word 'atoll' comes from the *Dhivehi* word *atholhu*) of the archipelago is enclosed by a coral reef, which is cut by many deep, natural channels. The reef structure peculiar to Maldives, known as *faru* (another *Dhivehi* word taken into English), consists of a line of circular reefs. Around each island a protective reef encloses a lagoon, although some are difficult to reach by boat. Small and low-lying, most of the islands can be walked across in ten minutes; few are longer than two kilometres, and the longest is eight kilometres. Few again are much higher than two metres, and the highest is no more than three metres above sea-level.

Thus the islands are vulnerable to wind and sea. The barrier reefs protect the islands from storms and waves, but this does not prevent some from being washed away. Strong currents flow between the atolls, swinging round with the monsoon winds. In 1812 and again in 1955, terrible storms devastated many of the northern islands. In 1964, the island of Hagngnaameedhoo, in Alifu Atoll (Ari Atoll), was inundated by high seas and in 1987 severe storms flooded the capital, Malé, and many other islands. If, as some scientists predict, the sea level continues to rise as a result of global warming, then within fifty years, Maldives, with its ancient and unique culture, could all be swept away.

Exactly how atolls are formed is still unclear. In 1842, after studying atolls in the Pacific and Atlantic oceans, Charles Darwin suggested that an atoll was created when volcanic land emerged from the sea and a coral reef grew around its edge. As it sank gradually back into the sea, it left the coral reefs encircling a shallow water-filled basin. Later, islands were formed as currents and tides swept coral debris onto sand bars, and eventually these were colonized by plants and trees.

Most scientists accept Darwin's theory although, in a postscript to his work on coral reefs, he added that there was something special about the islands of Maldives. More recently, Hans Hass suggested that over thousands of years platforms of coral reefs may have built up on top of the submerged mountain chain in the Indian Ocean until they rose above the surface. As coral is porous and unstable, the platforms sagged in the middle, leaving a ring of the hardest and highest coral (the rim of the atoll) where debris and sand accumulated and vegetation took hold to form Maldives.

The plant colonization of the islands tends to follow a common pattern. Along the beach, the first hardy pioneers are salt-resistant and small. Advancing inland, these are succeeded by a littoral hedge and secondly a thicket, which rarely exceeds five metres. In the centre, where rainwater reduces the salinity and soil evolves, there is thicker, more productive vegetation, similar to the lowland tropical rainforest

Above: One of many limestone sculptures found amid the ruins of a vast temple complex on Nilandhoo Island in Faafu Atoll (North Nilandhoo Atoll). It was probably buried as a votive offering to the Hindu god Shiva since many phallic lingam *sculptures have been unearthed nearby.*

of Sri Lanka. This consists mainly of coconut palms, banyan, screwpine, vines, and mangroves. Coconut trees often grow down to the water's edge.

In such a harsh environment, it is perhaps not surprising that the total flora only adds up to about 600 species, half of which are cultivated plants. The number of fully naturalized species is fewer than 260; probably fewer than 100 existed before the islands were settled. Animal life is equally sparse, with no more than a few grey herons, migratory frigatebirds, and flying foxes. Crows, a major nuisance in the northern atolls, were first introduced by seafarers who released them at sea to discover if land was near.

The tiny specks of land, separated by great stretches of water, that make up Maldives have long been a great puzzle. Just as the early history of the country is shrouded in mystery, so no one knows exactly how many islands exist in the archipelago. British Admiralty charts show some 1,100 islands, and a recent Maldives Government survey details 1,196. If sand bars and coral outcrops were included, the figure would be nearer 2,000.

The problem of counting them accurately is exacerbated by the fact that new ones come and old ones go. Islands also merge or split in two. Islets are constantly arising from the coral reefs and a 1955 storm in Shaviyani Atoll (North Miladhummadulu Atoll) created three new islands. Others slowly erode and vanish. Around 1960, for instance, the fairly large island of Feydhoo Finolhu in Malé Atoll vanished — washed away by erosion. Now the island has formed again, and is being used by the Ministry of Education in its school education programmes.

Officially, 202 of the islands are now inhabited, but many more show signs of past occupation. Some desert islands are used regularly by neighbouring islanders who collect firewood and coconuts, and even cultivate them.

Maldivians are totally in harmony with their maritime environment, for the sea is ever-constant. Yet, while it is the source of life and livelihood, it is also a capricious and volatile threat, awesome in its power. As with all seafarers, Maldivians carefully observe the patterns of nature around them and adapt their lives accordingly. Central to their existence is the weather, which determines when they go fishing, plant crops, or sail over the horizon.

Situated in the tropics, Maldives is hot and humid for most of the year. Temperatures are usually in the thirties and rarely drop below twenty-six degrees centigrade. Refreshing sea breezes, however, take the sting out of the sun except, perhaps, at midday when it reaches its zenith. The year is divided into two main seasons according to the monsoons: the north-east blows from November to April when, after some initially strong winds and squalls, the sky turns an endless blue and the sun shines from six in the morning to six at night. The wet south-west monsoon blows from May to November.

Average annual rainfall is 1,967 millimetres, although it is more variable in the south. Cloudbursts are often so heavy that the islands become awash with water. Yet, even in the rainy season, the tropical sun soon bursts through and quickly dries the coral sand.

Above: Elegant, flowing lines of Dhives Akuru *closely resemble the twelfth-century Sinhalese script* Elu. *Written from left to right, it is unlike the modern* Thaana *script — introduced in the late sixteenth century — which flows from right to left.*

Aware of the subtle changes in the island weather, Maldivians have developed their own complex calendar. Based on certain stars that wax and wane with either the sun or moon, their system, *nakaiy*, refers to any one of the twenty-eight seasonal divisions of the year and the clusters of stars that represent them. The origins of the calendar lie in India; the root of the word *nakaiy* is *nakshatra*, Sanskrit for star or heavenly body.

Maldivians use this calendar not only to determine the seasons for fishing and farming but also as an astrological system to predict the future, making it a fascinating combination of common sense, scientific observation, and downright superstition. Certain seasons, for instance, are considered auspicious times to dig a well, to start wearing jewellery, or to lay down the keel of a new boat.

Under the *nakaiy* system (each *nakaiy* lasts thirteen or fourteen days), the Maldivians divide the year into two distinct seasons: *hulhagu* and *iruvai*. *Hulhagu* (the south-west monsoon), which has eighteen *nakaiy*, is a period of strong winds and stormy weather. *Iruvai* (north-east monsoon), when the wind blows from the east, has nine *nakaiy*.

During the first *nakaiy* of the south-west monsoon (*assidha*) the first rains fall; if the Maldivians get themselves wet at this time it will bring them luck. The following *nakaiy* are good for clearing land and planting seeds. In late June, the sixth *nakaiy* (*adha*), seafarers steer towards the middle of the storm clouds as these often divide to give a clear path. Towards the end of the south-west monsoon, fishing is generally good. During the first period of the north-east monsoon season (*mula*) the sun shines and fishing is usually good on the eastern side of the northern atolls. And so it goes — nothing so much as this subtle and complex calendar so clearly shows the Maldivians' profound practical knowledge of nature and their careful adaptation to their environment.

Just as the exact number of islands in Maldives is an enigma, so its history remains a great puzzle. According to one legend, a single king ruled Maldives before the arrival of Islam. The story goes:

Once upon a time, when Maldives were still sparsely inhabited, a Prince of royal birth named Koimala Kaloa, *who had married the Ceylon King's daughter, made a voyage with her in two vessels from* Serendib Island. *Reaching the Maldives they were becalmed, and rested awhile at* Rasgetheemu Island *in North Malosmadulu Atol. The Maldive Islanders learning that the two chief visitors were of Ceylon royal descent invited them to remain; and ultimately proclaimed* Koimala *their King at* Rasgetimu, *the original 'King's Island'. Subsequently* Koimala *and his spouse migrated thence to* Male . . . *and settled there with the consent of the aborigines of* Giraavaru Island, *then the most important community of Male atoll.*

The legend says that this first king sent the two ships back to Sri Lanka to bring over other people of 'the Lion Race', whereupon his son 'reigned as a Buddhist for twelve years, and was then converted to Islam, ruling for thirteen years more before he finally departed for Mekka'. Then his daughter reigned as nominal sultana until her son 'married a lady of the country. From them, the subsequent Rulers of the Maldives were descended'. Clearly this account simply boils down many centuries of pre-Islamic history to one reign.

Although official Maldivian history does not begin before the twelfth century, there are many literary and archaeological clues to early times. Maldives was clearly a stopping-off point for some of the great seafaring civilizations that roamed the high seas well before European maritime history began. A Roman coin of 90 BC has been discovered in the archipelago. Since it was the Egyptians who taught the Romans how to cross the Indian Ocean, it may not be too fanciful to imagine the proud Egyptian papyrus ships sailing with their colourful square sails along the highway of the sun through the Equatorial Channel. Perhaps Maldivian men modelled the elegantly curved bows of their boats after the Egyptians, and the women the beautifully embroidered collar pieces of their dresses.

Early seafarers made fairly accurate estimates of the number of islands in the archipelago. The first reference to Maldives, made by the Greek geographer Ptolemy in the second century AD, is to '1,378 little islands' west of Taprobane (Sri Lanka). Pappus of Alexandria, who lived at the end of the fourth century, follows Ptolemy and mentions Taprobane and '1,370 adjacent islands'. Scholasticus, the Theban who lived about the same time and visited the Malabar Coast, mentions the 'thousand islands' and commented on their treacherous nature since they had 'loadstone rocks which attract iron-bound vessels to their destruction'.

Among the great Arab travellers who crossed the Indian Ocean, the Persian Sulaiman the Merchant, who lived in the ninth century, wrote: 'In the sea known as sea of Herkend there are nearly 1,900 islands', adding that 'the ruler of these islands is a woman', and that their wealth consisted of cowries. El Mas'udi, the Arab traveller who visited Sri Lanka at the beginning of the tenth century, claimed that between the sea of Herkend and the sea of Lar, there were many separate islands: 'There are 2,000 counted islands here. To be more accurate there are 1,900 islands here.'

The Chinese, of course, were great navigators. Dating perhaps from the fifth century BC, the *Shu-Ching* or *Classic History* mentions 'Weak Waters', in the area. Fah-Hian who visited Sri Lanka about the year AD 412 mentioned the small islands below it. After travelling with Cheng Ho's great expedition to East Africa in 1433, Ma Huan stated in *The Overall Survey of the Ocean's Shores* that the Maldive Islands were the 'Three Thousand Weak Waters' referred to by tradition. He not only lists identifiable islands but mentions how foreign ships come from every place to purchase ropes. Certainly, at the time of the Ming Dynasty (1368–1644), the Chinese had much knowledge of the submerged Liu-Shan (Liu-Mountains), as they called the archipelago, and its geography, climate, products, and customs.

The Europeans were latecomers to the Indian Ocean. In 1498, Vasco da Gama was the first to reach the Indian Ocean and nine years later Dom Lourenço de Almeida discovered Maldives for Portugal. When the French brothers Jean and Raoul Parmentier landed from their ships *Pensée* and *Sacré* on the southern island of Fua Mulaku in the Equatorial Channel they were warmly welcomed. The headman on the island particularly impressed them with his geography:

The chief Priest, who was a man of much discretion and knowledge . . . showed the Captain in what quarters lay the countries of Adam (Mesopotamia where Christians placed the Garden of Eden), Persia, Ormus, Calicut, Muluque and Sumatra; and proved himself to be both learned and well-travelled.

Such knowledge clearly reflects the wide extent of the islands' trading connections at the time.

These early literary references create a tantalizing picture of Maldives, but only now, as the nature of early Maldivian society begins to be discovered, is a more substantial one emerging. Recorded history only begins about the time of the conversion of Maldives to Islam in the year 583 of the Holy Prophet (AD 1153). As Christians in Europe begin their calendar from the birth of Christ and tend to dismiss all earlier religions as pagan, so Maldivians follow the Islamic calendar. Until recently they had little interest in what happened before. Not only was Maldivian pre-Islamic history suppressed but most pre-Muslim artefacts were destroyed. In this conservative society

Above: Demon face of five-sided stele discovered on Malé where monthly sacrifices of a virgin to a sea monster were said to take place. Carved from local limestone, these statues featured feline teeth, outstretched tongues, moustaches, top knots, and earlobes inserted with circular discs. The object is inscribed with the oldest script of Maldives, known as Eveyla Akuru.

Following pages: Causeways link tourist resorts in Malé Atoll with a neighbouring uninhabited island on the same coral plateau. There are some 1,190 islands in the Maldivian archipelago, about 200 of which are inhabited and more than seventy turned into resorts.

Above: Figures of a lion and demon probably decorated the frieze of a pre-Islamic temple on Nilandhoo Island. The human figure has the elongated earlobes and outstretched tongue of other 'demon statues' found in Maldives. The lion statue implies a link with the Buddhist Sinhalese of Sri Lanka, who called themselves the 'Lion People'. The first Muslims in Maldives smashed the old idols and razed the beautiful Buddhist and Hindu temples to the ground.

with Islamic ideals, the general feeling in the past was that it was better not to unearth what was buried.

Now, however, a new generation of Maldivian historians, sanctioned by politicians and religious leaders, has begun to explore the early period of Maldivian history in search of greater understanding of their country. Although their recorded history may be short, they now take pride in the fact that their real history is as old as their neighbours on the Indian subcontinent.

The first person to make a study of pre-Islamic history in Maldives was the British civil servant H. C. P. Bell, who first landed on Maldives when he was shipwrecked in 1879. Later he returned to investigate 'the pre-existence of Buddhism in the Group'. The monographs of this Commissioner of the Ceylon Civil Service show a great love of his subject.

During his visits in the early 1920s, Bell recorded many archaeological sites in the outlying atolls. In particular, he came across many large rounded mounds of coral stone and rubble, known locally as *hawittas,* which he thought were the remains of ancient *stupas*

similar to the Buddhist *dagoba* temples in Sri Lanka. With local help, he excavated some of these *hawittas* and found many Buddhist statues, thus confirming his view that Maldives must have been Buddhist before its conversion to Islam. He also came across statues of the Hindu god Shiva, and other artefacts which suggest that Hinduism from south India must have been influential there. Although Bell was little more than an amateur, he left a unique record of much curious archaeological, historical, and cultural data.

Many *hawittas* that Bell recorded still stand, although perhaps only half their original size as local villagers have used the stone for building. On many islands the mounds are also called *hatteli*, meaning 'seven cooking pots', probably referring to the seven superimposed spire-like kettles found on Buddhist *dagobas* in Sri Lanka.

When asked who they think built the *hawittas*, the islanders inevitably reply the Redin. But who were the Redin? There is no evidence to suggest who they really were. But most probably, Redin were the Buddhists who lived in the country prior to its conversion to Islam.

Whoever they were, the Redin dedicated an enormous amount of effort, skill, and wealth to build their temples in these remote islands. They were not only great builders but phenomenal sailors. One legend tells how the Redin once cooked their food on an island in the north only to travel to another island in the south to eat it.

Further light was shed on the Maldivian puzzle in the early 1980s when President Maumoon Gayoom invited Thor Heyerdahl of Kon Tiki fame to investigate some of the archaeological sites in the country. Heyerdahl — accompanied by Mohamed Ibrahim Loutfi, then member of the National Advisory Council of the National Centre for Linguistic and Historical Research — visited many locations recorded by Bell and, following local advice, also discovered new ones.

In his travels, Heyerdahl found some marvellous examples of superb craftsmanship — particulary on the islands of Fua Mulaku, Gan and Vaadhoo.

From archaeological records, it is clear that Buddhists and, to a lesser extent Hindus, came to the archipelago before it was converted to Islam. In the past, historians argued that Maldivians were a mixture of Dravidians from southern India and Sinhalese from Sri Lanka.

Recent evidence, however, suggests that the picture is more complex. There may well have been links with the Naga and Yakka people who developed the pre-Buddhist civilization in Sri Lanka. Hindu Tamils from southern India may have crossed over. Following the arrival of these two cultures, Aryans from north-west India could have settled in Maldives at the same time that they colonized Sri Lanka, although Sinhalese Buddhists undoubtedly came from Sri Lanka at a later date.

While the principal cultural affinities of Maldivians are with the Sinhalese, there is undoubtedly a Tamil substratum. In Maldives a man-beast myth that exists to explain the origin of the people is very close to the Sinhalese myth of the 'Lion People'. At the same time, the Giraavaru people claim descent from Tamils.

Whatever the exact pattern of settlement may have been, the great variety of physical characteristics found in Maldives suggests that

Above: One of several copperplates recording the official history of the early sultans. It dates from the late twelfth century and was written in the ancient script Eveyla Akuru. *The Maldivian language —* Dhivehi *— belongs to the Indo-Iranian group of languages.*

Above: Old Maldivian currency, consisting of the Rufiyaa *which is divided into 100* laari. *For centuries, taxes were paid to the sultan in cowries which were also exported to be used as small change in the countries bordering the Indian Ocean.*

independent groups of people reached these islands in prehistoric times. Later, Indonesians, Malays, Arabs, and Africans all added to the racial and cultural melting pot.

Islam, however, is central to the life of all Maldivians. The law is based on the Muslim code of *shari'a* as interpreted by a judge (*gazi*), which applies the principles of the Qur'an to society. Indeed, like all Muslims, Maldivians do not distinguish between law and religion; *shari'a,* the nearest word for law, means the way, the true path of religion.

The main events and festivals of Maldivian life follow the Muslim calendar. From the age of three, a child is taught the Arabic alphabet, recites extracts from the Qur'an, and learns the basic principles and history of Islam. As they grow older, they will be expected to offer prayers with the family. On Fridays, boys dress in their best clothes and go with their father to the local mosque; girls go with their mother to a mosque specially for women, if there is one, or pray at home. When they grow up the ambition of all pious Maldivians is to make the pilgrimage to Mecca.

Belonging to the largest and most traditional Islamic sect, the Sunnis, Maldivians believe that 'There is no God but Allah', confident that he is one, supreme, and all powerful. Islam means literally 'surrender to God'. Muslims also believe that Muhammad is the messenger of Allah. In a long line of prophets, including Adam, Noah, Abraham, Moses, David, Solomon, and Jesus, Muhammad is considered the last and greatest. He is not regarded as divine — the archangel Gabriel brought him the message of Allah — but he is the best of men.

At the same time, Maldivians follow the liberal Shafi'ite school, founded by Al-Shafi'i, an Arab-born Persian descended from the Qurayish tribe who generally gave equal weight to the Qur'an and to the words and deeds of the Prophet Muhammad as written down in the Hadith. In some of his interpretations of the principles of Islam, he preferred to rely on the latter. The Maldivians, therefore, share similar beliefs to those Muslims living in the East Indies, East Africa, lower Egypt, and southern Arabia.

All Maldivians believe in afterlife and in the final judgement which decides whether they go to hell or heaven. Only right conduct can assure the latter, and that means keeping to the five pillars of their religion: to repeat the creed 'There is no God but Allah, and Muhammad is the Prophet of Allah' (*La ilaha illa Allah, Muhammad rasul Allah*); to say prayers five times a day (at dawn, midday, mid-afternoon, sunset, and after darkness); to give alms to the poor; to make a pilgrimage to Mecca if possible once in a lifetime; and to fast during the month of Ramadan (*Roadha Mas*).

The key events of the year are all Muslim religious feasts and festivals. During Ramadan, everyone except those too young or sick (including pregnant and menstruating women) are meant to abstain from all food, water, cigarettes, and sex from sunrise to sunset for a lunar month.

At sundown, the sound of a hornshell signals the end of the day's fast; all rush to drink the juice of the young coconut or tea and to enjoy

Opposite: Tourist complex superimposed during the last decade on a desert island in Malé Atoll. Over millions of years currents and waves deposited coral debris to form a sand spit above the water which was slowly colonized by salt-resistant plants and crowned by coconut palms.

Above: In the capital Malé, the tomb of Muhammad Thakurufaanu, one of Maldives' most famous heroes.

snacks while waiting for the piles of specially prepared rice and curried fish to be served. The next day, they wake before dawn to eat their last bite until evening. A long, dry, and hungry day stretches before them. The month of fasting comes to an end when the new moon rises and is celebrated by a great feast called *Kuda Id* when every family sacrifices a precious chicken and rejoices with much merriment and good cheer.

Within the family, the main occasions are those associated with birth and death. A child is named when it is seven days old and friends gather to wish the child well and listen to an Islamic recital called *Mawloodh*, followed by a feast. When a member of the family dies, prayers are said at the graveside and in the house for a week or more. The memorial service, or *faathihaiy*, is held forty days later, with more recitals and food — something that can be repeated on the same day for several generations if the person is sufficiently important to be so remembered.

Despite their faith, Maldivians are extremely superstitious. They believe in supernatural beings called *dhevi*. Almost certainly this belief antedates Islam for many of the words used to describe them are from Sanskrit and Pali. The scholar Hassan Ahmed Maniku has suggested that a *dhevi* refers to:

the idea of an invisible, but sometimes visible being, capable of moving across the high seas, land and even through barriers. It may be helpful or harmful. It may require supplication, rebuke or even sacrifice.

To describe the *dhevi*, Maldivians often use the Arabic word *jinni* — in Islam these belong to a third group of created beings, apart from the humans and angels, said to be made of fire and possessing superhuman powers who will be called to account with humans on the Judgement Day. There is a story that when a student told his Islamic professor in Egypt that he was from Maldives, the venerable scholar replied; 'Ah, that is where Allah has exiled all the *jinnis* of the whole world.'

The British naval officers I. A. Young and Wilmott Christopher, who visited Maldives in the mid-nineteenth century, observed that 'the most absurd and superstitious fancies exert a powerful and pernicious influence' on the people. Certainly they believe that spirits live all around them in nature: in the sea, in the sky, in the trees, and in the rain.

Hassan Maniku even argues that primitive Maldivian society managed to produce 'a religion of its own'. While throughout the centuries many of these beliefs have been condemned by the Islamic authorities, they betray remarkable originality and vision and form a unique treasury of folklore and stories.

Islanders see no conflict between their belief in Islam and *dhevi*. To ward off the evil eye and to keep evil spirits at bay, they often listen to lengthy recitals from the Qur'an and other Arabic texts. When extraordinary events occur, many turn to the local wise man immersed in *fanditha*, a special knowledge that is part science, part magic. He is consulted when the rains fail, the fishing is poor, or a woman is barren. With potions and charms, the *fanditha* man calls on the spirits to resolve the problems. In an uncertain world where the unknown is feared, a belief in *fanditha* gives Maldivians a sense of control over their destiny.

Many different stories and spirits are connected with the *dhevi*. During

Above: Tombstones of important personages in Koaganu cemetery on Meedhoo Island (Seenu Atoll).

Opposite: Bath adjoining Kedeyre Mosque on Fua Mulaku Island (Gnaviyani Atoll). The different-sized stones of the walls of the filled bath are built with a precision and skill known to only a few master masons in the ancient world.

his stay in the fifteenth century, François Pyrard de Laval noted that Maldivians believed in:

a king of the sea, to who in like sort they make prayers and ceremonies while on a voyage; or when they go fishing, they dread above all things to offend the kings of the winds and of the sea. So, too, when they are at sea, they durst not spit nor throw anything to windward for fear lest he should be offended, and with like intent they look abaft.

Many fishermen still believe in a *dhevi* called Odivaru Ressi who lives in the sea, and harms fishing boats, fishermen, bait, and fish, although the *dhevi* is also sometimes benevolent. The spirit manifests itself overhead as a long dark or red shadow, or as a sailfish, black marlin, or wahoo. The *dhevi* that takes possession of a boat ruins the fishing and makes the body itch.

The *dhevi* called Vigani, which inhabits the seas and may be seen on water near the horizon, is the lord of death. Some describe this spirit as a small man, or greyish monkey with thick coat. Vigani is also believed to have a long trunk, like an elephant, which it uses to suck food from the graves of the dead. Vigani is said to be the cause of sudden death and major epidemics. Hassan Maniku observes:

In some islands when too many people die suddenly, Fanditha *men look for signs and determine the cause to be from Vigani by looking at the sunset and the crimson clouds on the west. If a small compact cloud in the shape of a fish is seen glowing, then the cause of death is attributed to Vigani. He then performs* Fanditha *and tries to cut the cloud into pieces. If he is unable to do this, it means that the entire community will be obliterated. Then the community has to move to another island and settle there.*

The spiritual leader of all *dhevi*, Buddevi, lives in thick jungles, on the beach, and around abandoned houses. Buddevi, who is believed to appear where the water drips from coconut leaves after a shower of rain, may be seen as a cat or well-built man. It is said that whoever sees this malevolent *dhevi* falls ill.

Like their popular beliefs, the roots of the unique *Dhivehi* language reflect the complex origins of the Maldivian people. Modern scholars consider *Dhivehi* to belong to the Indo-Iranian language group, closest to ancient Sinhala, with its links to Sanskrit and other ancient tongues from north-west India. At the same time, there are some elements of Tulu from the Malabar Coast of southern India; many words relating to the sea and the family, for instance, have Tamil roots.

There are three known scripts. The oldest is *Eveyla Akuru* (Ancient Letters) which is found in the first three copperplates dating from 1195 to 1238. This style evolved in the fourth copperplate of 1356–7 and is known as *Dhives Akuru*. Written from left to right, it is very close to Elu, the Sinhala script of the twelfth century, and its beautifully flowing form can be seen on old tombstones.

A third script, introduced in the mid-fifteenth century, came to be used throughout the islands. Known as *Thaana*, it is written like Arabic and Persian from right to left. Less cumbersome than the old script, it shows the influence of the Semitic mode of writing. There are only twenty-four letters in the alphabet, nine of which are derived from Arabic numerals. Vowels are represented simply by marks below or above a letter.

Like Latin in sixteenth-century Europe, Arabic was also spoken and written by the cultivated for the affairs of religion and science. In this century, however, English has become more important than Arabic as a second language, and in recent times a Latinized version of *Dhivehi* with English pronunciation has been introduced.

After the arrival of Islam in the twelfth century, the history of Maldives is clearer but the records are still few. Undoubtedly, the *Koimala* legend that founds the royal dynasty in Maldives is foreshortened by many centuries, but it underlies the close link with Sri Lanka and recognizes the existence of Buddhism in the archipelago before Islam. The official story is taken up in the *Tarikh*, a history of Maldivian sultans from 1153 (the date of the Islamic conversion) to 1821.

There exists, however, another copperplate, called the *Isdhoo loamaafaana*, which begins in the year AD 1105 (505 AH), when 'the great King, *Sri Maanaabarana* of the house of *Theemu*, the Lord of the Lunar Dynasty became the King of this country'. It then lists the names of the four Buddhist kings before Islam came to the islands and the length of their reign.

From the twelfth century, the Arabs most influenced the course of Maldivian history. They had been plying the Indian Ocean centuries before Vasco da Gama first rounded the tip of Africa 500 years ago. Maldives, or 'Dibajat' as they called it, was a strategic entrepôt lying on the sea routes to Malacca and China. The Arab seafarers landed for water and dried fish and coconuts and often stayed long enough to enjoy the pleasures of a temporary wife. Maldivians had long been famous for their easygoing ways, no doubt unconsciously recognizing the benefit of new blood in their close-knit communities.

The Arabs also took on board sacks of cowrie shells, which were to be

Above: Beautifully carved tombstone with an epitaph written in Dhives Akuru.

Above: Traditionally, Islamic tombstones with a short stub are for men and round ones for women. The epitaph is carved in Arabic.

found in abundance in the lagoons of the islands, as ballast for their return voyage. Throughout the Indian Ocean in medieval times cowries were used as small change, and Maldivian cowries have been found as far north as the Arctic Circle in Norway, and as far west as Mali.

Visiting Arab traders brought Islam to Maldives in 1153–4. It was an Arab who converted the Buddhist king, Theemugey Maha Kaliminja, to their religion. The story goes that one Abu al Barakaath arrived in Maldives in 1153 only to find a 'colony of ignorant idolators'.

By managing to exorcise the demon god Rannamaari, who came from the sea on Malé Island every full moon to rape and kill a local virgin who was offered as a sacrifice, he won the gratitude and admiration of all. He accomplished this feat by dressing as a girl and spending all night reading the Qur'an. It was all too much for the sea monster which departed, never to return. The sultan was so impressed that he converted to Islam and persuaded his subjects to follow suit. The old idols were broken and the temples razed to the ground.

The famous Arab traveller who relates the story, Ibn Battuta, read the hero's name as 'Abu al Barakaath Yusuf al Barbari' — from Berber land in North Africa — from the carved inscription in the Friday Mosque in Malé, thereby identifying him as one of his compatriots. Modern scholars, however, argue that it reads 'Al Tabreezi' — from Tabriz in Persia. It has also been suggested that it could even refer to Beruwela in Sri Lanka. Such scholastic debate, however, does not affect the veneration in which Abu al Barakaath Yusuf al Barbari is held. His grave on Malé is a holy shrine.

A more political interpretation of these events is that Maldives adopted the Islamic religion not because of some miracle in scaring away a supernatural being but because the ruling elite realized that they would be unable to hold Buddhist Sri Lanka at arm's length without the support of their powerful Islamic neighbours in the Indian Ocean. Certainly from the twelfth century Arab visitors were received with great hospitality, some of them even being appointed *gazis* (chief judges of the Islamic law) as well as sultans.

After embracing the Islamic faith in AD 1153, King Kaliminja became Sultan Dharmas Mohamed Ibn Abdulla and during the thirteen subsequent years of his reign strove to introduce Islamic law throughout the islands. He then decided to make the pilgrimage to Mecca and set sail, never to to be heard from again.

Not everybody converted to Islam immediately. It took almost three score years before the whole country became Muslim. According to the *loamaafaana*, the next king who came to power in AD 1179 had to send an expedition south to the island of Dhabidhoo in Laamu Atoll:

The Great King, Srimat Gadanaditya, *an ornament to the Lunar Dynasty, resplendent as gold, firm as an Asala [stone] pillar, defender of the entire hundred thousand of islands, brilliant as the sun, moon, and stars, virtuous in every manner, lord of love, mine of jewels, adorned with a crown set with gems — On the fourth year of his becoming the sole monarch he, having destroyed the shrine erected previously by the infidel kings of Dabuduv, uprooted the Buddha images, and caused the infidel Kings to read the* Shahaadhath *[a Muslim creed].*

The Theemuge, or Malei, dynasty was to rule through fifteen sultans for the next 190 years. This was followed by the Hilali dynasty, which had twenty-nine rulers reigning for a total of 170 years.

In Maldives, women have always played a significant role in politics and society. As nowadays in Minicoy of the neighbouring Lakshadweep Islands, it seems that matrilineal inheritance was well-established in early times. The country may also have been ruled by matriarchy. Early Arabic records mention that before converting to Islam, the islands were ruled by a queen. Sulaiman the Merchant and Al-Mas'udi at the turn of the tenth century both record this fact. At the beginning of the twelfth century, Al-Adrisi wrote:

It has always been a custom with them that a woman arbitrate, a custom from which they do not depart. This queen is called Dmhra. She wears garments of woven gold, and her headwear is a crown of gold studded with various kinds of rubies and precious stones. She wears gold sandals.

In these islands nobody wears sandals, except this queen alone, and if anyone is found wearing sandals, his feet are amputated.

Above: Impressive ruins of a pre-historic Buddhist stupa *on the island of Isdhoo at the most northerly tip of Laamu Atoll. These mounds scattered throughout the archipelago are known as* hawittas. *Over the centuries, their beautiful dressed stones have been much plundered by the locals for various purposes. Towering over the coconut trees, gleaming white in the Equatorial sun, in its heyday this temple would have been a famous landmark for mariners sailing through the channel between the atolls.*

Overleaf: British schooner anchored off Bandos Island in Malé Atoll. The wrecks of many vessels scattered on the coral reefs are testimony to the uncharted dangers of sailing in the Maldivian archipelago.

Top: Beautiful Maldivian girl on Isdhoo Island in Laamu Atoll.

Above: Henna-painted fingernails of this young woman betray her family's Arabian past.

On ceremonial occasions, and the feast-days of her sect, this queen rides with her slave-girls behind her, in full procession of elephants, banners and trumpets, while the king and all other ministers follow her at a distance. . . .

With the coming of Islam, women were obliged to take a back seat as no woman can be a religious leader. Nevertheless, unlike other Muslim states, Maldives has had several sultanas. One of the most memorable was Sultana Khadeeja Rehendi Kabaidhi Kilege, who ruled on three separate occasions between 1342 and 1380. She was not one to be balked. She came to power after the banishment of her younger brother, and again in 1364 following the death of her first husband, who had deposed her and ruled for a year. In 1373, she was overthrown again, this time by her second husband, but three years later she apparently killed him and succeeded to the throne for the third time. Triumphant over the dead bodies of her treacherous husbands, she ruled alone until her death in 1380.

It was during her rule, in 1344, that Ibn Battuta, one of many Arab traders landing for provisions and for the cowrie shells that formed the currency in southern India and Africa, came to the islands. His is the earliest descriptive account of the Maldive islands and their inhabitants.

Battuta remained about ten months on Malé and left a detailed account of the condition of the islands, their government, their customs, and their religion. He noted how Maldives exported dried fish and coir rope to India, China, and Yemen. The Bengalis took cowrie shells in exchange for rice, while the Yemenite traders took them as ballast for their ships.

Battuta left a very favourable picture of the country at the time:

The people of the Maldives are upright and pious, sound in belief and sincere in thought; their bodies are weak, they are unused to fighting, and their armour is prayer. Once when I ordered a thief's hand to be cut off, a number of those in the room fainted. The Indian pirates do not raid or molest them, as they have learned from experience that anyone who seizes anything from them speedily meets misfortune.

The sultana's army of about 1,000 men consisted of people from both Malé and the islands, and they were paid monthly in rice.

Battuta was particularly attracted to the women and made full use of the custom that 'any newcomer could marry if he so desired, then on leaving he simply repudiated his wife'. It is easy to get married in these islands, he noted:

on account of the smallness of the dowries and the pleasure of their women's society. When ships arrive, the crew marry wives, and when they are about to set sail they divorce them. It is really a sort of temporary marriage. The women never leave the country.

It was common for young girls to hire themselves out as servants to the wealthier families. It was also usual to have slave-concubines — Ibn Battuta was given two.

Although Battuta was at first very well-received, he eventually fell out with Sultana Khadeeja's husband, the *wazir* (prime minister), who

feared his growing influence and resented his haughty independence. After marrying the sultana's mother-in-law — 'one of the best of women' — Battuta became *gazi* and imposed a strict interpretation of Islamic Law. He changed the practice of divorced wives staying in the houses of their former husbands, enforced on pain of public beating the observance of Friday prayers, and tried, unsuccessfully, to make the women cover the top part of their body. As the *gazi*, he received the entire income of three islands. His marriage to three other well-connected wives soon confirmed the *wazir*'s fears that he was becoming too powerful. After about ten months, Battuta had had enough and decided to set sail for Malabar.

On his way, he stayed in Mulaku Island of Meemu Atoll (Mulaku Atoll) in the south. Although there for only seventy days he found the time to marry two wives. Eventually he left on 22 August 1344, but not without regret. Like so many travellers since, he had a final glimpse of the magic that brings so many under the spell of Maldives. He came across a tiny island where a weaver and his family lived alone:

And I swear I envied that man, and wished that the island had been mine, that I might have made it my retreat until the inevitable hour should befall me.

Battuta returned to Maldives only once, to see his son, but he decided to leave him with his mother.

At this time, trade with the Indian subcontinent was largely in the hands of Maamali Marakkaaru, a Muslim merchant from the south-west coast of India who had such a stranglehold over trade that he was known as the 'Lord of the Maldive Islands'.

The Portuguese mariners and traders who followed Vasco da Gama into the Indian Ocean demanded a share in the profitable Indian Ocean trade routes. In particular, they were impressed by the Maldivian trade. In 1503, cruising off Calicut, Vincent Sodré, Vasco da Gama's commander, came across some Maldivian ships. A chronicler relates:

When he was off Calicut, he sighted four sails, which he overhauled and took. They proved to be gundras, *barques of the Maldive islands. . . .* Gundras *are built of palm timber, joined and fastened with pegs of wood without any bolts. The sails are made of mats of the dry leaves of the palm. These vessels were laden with coir and cowrie . . . good store of silks, both coloured and white, of divers fabrics and qualities, and many brilliant tissues of gold, made by the islanders themselves, who get the silk, gold, and cotton-thread from the numerous ships that pass among the islands on their way from the coast of Bengal to the Straits of Mecca. There ships buy these stuffs from the islanders, supplying them in exchange with the materials whereof they are made. Thus are these islands a great emporium for all parts, and the Moors of India frequent them, bartering their salt and earthenware, which are not made at the islands, and also rice and silver.*

In 1517, Sultan Kalu Muhammad entered into a treaty with the Portuguese. They established a trading post in Malé but it was burnt down the following year by the Maldivians with help from corsairs

Above: Young boy proudly holds a skipjack tuna, part of the day's catch harvested by his father and fellow islanders. Until recently, tuna was the mainstay of the Maldivian economy.

from Malabar. In response, the Portuguese sent an armada under the command of Joao Gomes Cheiradinheiro, who landed in Malé with 120 men and built a fort.

The next sultan, Hassan IX, was impressed by the Portuguese and travelled to Cochin in India in 1551 to find out more about Christianity. On New Year's Day, 1552, he became a Christian and was baptized. Two years later he married a Christian lady from Goa. Keen to convert his ministers and chiefs to Christianity, Hassan invited them to Cochin. Instead, they seized two expeditions of loyal subjects which tried to reach him.

It was not until 1558 that a third expedition, led by Captain Andreas Andre, reached Cochin. The Portuguese then returned to take over the country from Sultan Ali VI who had been in power for only two and a half months. He was killed in the struggle and his death is now a national anniversary celebrated as 'Martyr's Day'. The Portuguese then ruled through Andreas Andre, known locally as Adiri Adiri. The *Tarikh* relates:

The Maldivians then submitted to Captain Adiri Adiri, who proclaimed himself 'Sultan'. He sent Christians to take charge in all parts of the Maldives, and enforced submission. The Portuguese ruled most cruelly for several years, committing intolerable enormities. The sea ran red with Muslim blood, the people were sunk in despair. At this juncture God Almighty moved the heart of Khatib Muhammad, son of Khatib Hussain of Utimu . . . to fight with the Infidels and to end the crying wrongs. Praying to God for wisdom to conquer, he took council with his younger brothers.

After eight years of guerrilla war, the three sons of the island chief of Utheemu eventually led a successful rebellion, although one son was killed in the process. The rebels landed on Malé, massacring the Portuguese community of more than 300, the night before a Portuguese deadline for all inhabitants to become Christians or face the death penalty.

In 1573, Muhammad Thakurufaanu, the second son of the chief of Utheemu, was declared sultan, founding the Utheemu dynasty that reigned for 132 years through seven rulers. He is now revered as the 'national hero' for his role in the country's fight to regain independence. Never again was Maldives ruled by a foreign power.

However, not all subsequent rulers were benevolent. Frenchman François Pyrard de Laval, the purser who was shipwrecked and taken prisoner for five years in 1602 when the *Corbin* ran onto a reef, left a fascinating and detailed account of the actions of the country's arbitrary ruler of the time. During his captivity, he learned broken *Dhivehi* and his three-volume work published in 1619 is a mine of curious contemporary information about Maldives and remains the most valuable period reference to the country. Only when a ship from Chittagong in Bengal arrived intent on salvaging the cannon on board the *Corbin* was Pyrard able to escape. Armaments were more important than men.

One of the last rulers of the Utheemu dynasty was Sultan Ibrahim Iskandar I, who ruled from 1648 to 1687. During his reign, he repelled several pirate expeditions from south India, built the Malé Friday

Mosque and minaret, and introduced many new customs. However, he became obsessed with a beautiful slave girl, Mariam Kabaafaanu. The son she bore him was chosen as the sultan's successor.

As he was only six when he became sultan, the affairs of the state were administered by a committee of *wazirs*. However, the young sultan's mother was able to influence the *wazirs* and seized power for herself. She then took a succession of lovers and encouraged the women of her court to do likewise. She met her death in a fashion as dramatic as her rise to power. Sailing to meet her victorious fleet after it had repulsed a pirate armada from Malabar in southern India, she ordered the gunners to fire a salute of cannon in the fleet's honour, but a spark fell on the powder magazine and the royal vessel blew up. Her body was never recovered and, soon after, her son died.

During the seventeenth century the Dutch ousted the Portuguese as the principal force in the Indian Ocean. In 1645, Maldives established diplomatic ties with the Dutch Governor of Sri Lanka and exchanged gifts — a practice that continued for two centuries. In return for cowrie shells, the Dutch provided a yearly supply of spices, areca-nut, and ammunition.

The Maldivians, however, still caused their own waves. After attacking Minicoy, then part of the Maldive islands, the Ali Raja retaliated. Landing in Malé in 1753, he carried away Sultan Mukkarram Muhammad Imaadhudhdheen III and destroyed the palace. But within weeks a local uprising, led by Gazi Hassan Izzuddeen, combined with the sudden appearance of a small French fleet, put to rest any designs on the islands that the Ali Rajas might have had. After their departure, Izzuddeen ruled in the name of the last sultan, but he came to the throne himself in 1759 after the death of Imaadhudhdheen III in Minicoy, thereby founding the Huraage dynasty that lasted 201 years through thirteen rulers until the country became a republic. Huravee Day is now a national holiday.

The trade relations of Maldives have always been far and extensive. Ibn Battuta records in the fourteenth century how they traded their fish and coir to India, China, and Yemen. But it was the simple cowrie shells from Maldives which reached the farthest countries. As early as 1500 BC some were placed in burial sites in the Indus Valley harbour city of Lothal. By AD 600 Maldives cowries had reached the Atlantic coast of Arctic Norway. In the early eleventh century the Arab traveller Al-Biruni recorded that the archipelago was called the 'Cowrie Islands'. Three centuries later Ibn Battuta came across them in Mali in West Africa.

The Maldivians cultivated cowries on palm leaves cast into the sea. They bartered them for rice from the people of Bengal who used them as money, as well as to sailors from Yemen, who used them as ballast in their ships. Ma Huan, a Chinese Muslim who travelled with Cheng Ho's celebrated 1433 expedition to East Africa, noted in the book he wrote on his return that Maldive cowries were sold in heaps in Thailand as well as Bengal. In 1563 the historian of Portuguese India, Joao de Barros, also noted how important Maldives cowries were in the maritime commerce of the day:

Above: In the prow of a traditional fishing dhoani, *pulled up on the beach for repairs, a young islander wields an* iloshi fathi, *a broom made from the thin flexible spines of coconut leaves.*

With these shells for ballast many ships are laden for Bengal and Siam, where they are used for money, just as we use small copper money for buying things of little value. And even to this kingdom of Portugal, in some years as much as two or three thousand quintals [100–150 tonnes] *are brought by way of ballast; they are then exported to Guinea, and the kingdoms of Benin and Congo, where they are used for money, the Gentiles of the interior in those parts making their treasure of it.*

From the eighteenth century, however, cowries began to lose their value as a medium of exchange in the Indian Ocean even though they continued to be used as common currency within the archipelago well into this century.

When the British took over from the Dutch in Sri Lanka in 1796, trade between Malé and Colombo increased. The sultan of that era, however, took himself a shade too seriously. In a letter to the Governor asking Sri Lanka not to tolerate anyone hostile to Maldives, and to take care of any Maldivian who was shipwrecked, he introduced himself thus:

Hail! The glorious, renowned, most wise, nobly-born ruler, comparable to the moon and the sun, the heroic warrior Sultan Hasan Nur-ud-din Iskandar, the warrior, the great King of the earth, to the King styled the Governor in Colombo, many thousand greetings from here.

Ultimately, Sri Lanka became the main purchaser of the principal export of Maldives — dried tuna fish. By the mid-nineteenth century, however, the archipelago was nearly bankrupt. Borah merchants from India rapidly came to dominate the economy, monopolizing the import and export trade, which consisted mainly of rice, sugar, cotton, dried fish, coconuts, and occasionally tortoiseshell. One company in particular — Kareemjee Jaufarujee — gained almost complete control of the economy and in 1887 resentment reached such a head that a group of locals led by businessmen burnt down the company's stores and godowns on Malé.

To end the troubles, on 16 December 1887 the young Sultan Muhammad Mu'in-uddin II signed a treaty with the British Governor of Sri Lanka under which Maldives Islands became a British Protectorate. In return for sovereignty over the islands, Britain pledged itself to protect the country against foreign enemies — and refrain from interfering in local affairs and administration.

Yet the turbulent political history of Maldives continued in the twentieth century with plot and counterplot. In 1932, Muhammad Shamsuddeen III, who had been recognized by the British over his rival, was obliged to accept the first written constitution in Maldivian history. It severely limited his powers and also introduced the principle of elections. Shamsuddeen III was deposed and Hassan Nooraddeen II became the first elected sultan.

During the Second World War, the British established two airstrips, one at Gan (Gamu) to the south in Laamu Atoll and the other at Kelai to the north in Haa Alifu Atoll (North Thiladhunmathee Atoll), to protect their strategic Indian Ocean interests. Three years after the war

Above: Plying the waters of the islands just as it has done for centuries, the traditional lateen-sailed dhoani *serves as a welcome 'water taxi' for locals and tourists alike.*

ended Sri Lanka achieved independence. In signing a 1948 defence pact, the Maldivian government allowed the British control of the islands' foreign affairs but no right to interfere in internal affairs.

Although the Maldivian constitution was rewritten in 1942, the sultan was forced to abdicate the following year. Abdul Majeed Didi — then Prime Minister and later advisor to the government — was then elected the ninety-third Sultan of Maldives, but he declined to accept and soon retired to Colombo where he died. In the event, Prime Minister Muhammad Amin Didi assumed almost complete control, introducing a modernization programme which included a National Security Service and establishing a government monopoly over the export of fish.

In 1953 the Sultanate was abolished and Amin Didi became Maldives' first President. Food shortages and his controversial ban on smoking tobacco, however, led to riots and he was subsequently arrested, dying in the village on Kurumba Island (Vihamanaafushi Island) soon after.

In turn, the newly written republican constitution was abolished

Above: Student in a modern single-sex secondary school in the capital Malé where the main language of tuition is English. Although living in an Islamic country, Maldivian women have traditionally played an important role in the nation's affairs.

and in 1954 Muhammad Farid Didi, the son of Abdul Majeed Didi, was elected to power — the ninety-fourth and last sultan of Maldives. Two years later the British negotiated a 100-year lease on their Gan air base which Premier Ibrahim Nasir, who came to power in 1957, revoked.

This aroused the anger of the islanders who lived on the three southernmost atolls. They had benefited from the presence of the British and now accused their government in Malé of treating them like serfs. In 1959 the three atolls ceded from Maldives to form the separate state of the United Suvadive Islands with Abdulla Afif Didi as President. The governing People's Council established a trading corporation and a bank.

In search of a solution to end the impasse, and perhaps also to buy time, Nasir agreed to a better deal with the British. In January 1962, however, he stealthily despatched a fleet of boats carrying armed men to invade the cessionist stronghold in the southern atolls, forcing Didi to flee to Seychelles. Nasir banished the other leaders to outlying islands and six years later was elected President of the second republic.

On 26 July 1965, Maldives joined the United Nations as a fully independent sovereign state. In 1968, after a referendum, the country once more adopted a Republican constitution. This was amended in 1972 to give the President far greater powers. The country's English name, Maldive Islands, was changed to the Republic of Maldives. The legal code remained based on the Islamic code of *shari'a*.

The administrative structure of Maldives, based on three tiers, is highly centralized and hierarchical. The administration of the inhabited islands, ruled by a local island chief (*katheeb*) and one or two deputies who work with an island council, is on the bottom tier. The island chief implements government policy and reports back on island affairs.

Atoll administration is on the second tier. For convenience, these have been grouped into nineteen atolls, each ruled by an appointed atoll chief (*atholhu verin*) and his deputies. The chief is responsible for the economic and political arrangements of the atoll. An Islamic judge deals with judicial matters by interpreting and applying the principles of *shari'a* to individual cases.

The top tier is occupied by the legislative body known as the Citizens' Majlis, consisting of forty-eight members, two elected from each atoll and Malé, and eight nominated by the President. The President, who is nominated by the Citizen's Majlis and confirmed by public referendum, holds supreme authority. As the Commander-in-Chief of the armed forces and Protector of Islam, he appoints cabinet ministers who need not necessarily be members of parliament.

Under this political system, Nasir, an authoritarian ruler, governed the country. Eventually he fell victim to his own ruthlessness. When Sri Lanka imposed foreign currency controls in 1972 the main market for Maldives' biggest export — dried fish — collapsed. The same year, tourism came to Maldives and Nasir was accused of using government cash to set up his own hotel and travel agency. The benefits of tourism did not reach many people. Inflation, spurred by oil prices, soared and in 1974 a large crowd protested against rising prices.

The following year, when Ahmed Zaki was elected as Prime Minister for a second term, Nasir banished him and other ministers in the hope of forestalling any attempt to remove him. He clung to power until 1978 before fleeing to Singapore with the greater part of the national exchequer. Maumoon Abdul Gayoom, then Minister of Transport, was elected as President and later Nasir, accused *in absentia* of corruption, was condemned to twenty-five years banishment and some of his properties were taken back by the government. He was later pardoned on 26 July 1990. Despite three coup attempts in 1980, 1983, and 1988, President Gayoom has remained in power.

Fishing is still the major industry, employing about forty per cent of the work force. The national company Maldive Shipping, managed from Singapore, operates more than forty tankers and vessels and handles ninety-five per cent of imports to Malé. Tourism has expanded most, however, and is now the major foreign exchange earner. Although social development has seen schools and health clinics develop on the outer atolls, Malé remains the hub of the widely scattered archipelago. While no one goes without food or shelter, Maldives remains one of the least developed countries in the world.

In recent years, the population has increased rapidly and Maldives is now the seventh most densely populated country on earth. In 1992, the citizens numbered over 230,000, a figure expected to increase to about 300,000 by the turn of the century. Yet apart from the critical overcrowding in Malé, this need not be a problem: there are nearly 1,000 uninhabited islands still to settle.

Standing at the crossroads of the Indian Ocean, the people of Maldives have had a long and chequered history. This, and their character, has long intrigued visitors. Early accounts tend to express the prejudices of the observers rather than provide an objective analysis, if such were possible. The French Parmentier brothers felt that they were 'poor-looking creatures', although their compatriot François Pyrard declared them to be 'quick and apprehensive, subtle and crafty'.

Not surprisingly, the Portuguese who tried to colonize the country in the sixteenth century held a low opinion; according to Duarte Barbosa, they were 'dull, feeble and malicious'. While admitting they were 'feeble folk', Joao Barros added 'but very clever; and above all they are mighty magicians'.

Since they had few defences from warlike visitors, Maldivians have always had to rely on guile to survive. They were fortunate in fostering the belief that if a seafarer stopping on their islands for water harmed them, then harm would befall the perpetrator as he continued his voyage. As Battuta put it, 'their armour is prayer'.

The British, who became their protectors in the nineteenth century, were both attracted by their peacefulness and repelled by their apparent apathy. Captain Moresby, who undertook a maritime survey between 1834 and 1836 for the British Admiralty, observed that the Maldivians 'always treated us with kindness and respect, yet with shyness and suspicion, supposing our motives'. His assistants, Lieutenants I. A. Young and Wilmott Christopher of the Indian Navy, left an interesting account of their stay, but they too reported that they were 'a quiet, peaceable race, hospitable and kind to strangers, though suspicious and distrustful of them'. Both attitudes, of course, were a product of island life. Nearly all commentators have remarked on the

Above: Members of the National Security Service of this island nation.

Above: Young women as well as men don police uniform in the Republic of Maldives.

Maldivians' superstitious nature, of their fear of spirits and *jinni* despite their faith in Islam.

The British civil servant and antiquarian H.C.P. Bell wrote in 1922 that 'a delightful spirit of ease and contentment seems to prevail universally', although he stressed their insularity, even in the capital Malé; it 'desires nothing so greatly as to be left by the outside world as much as possible alone, to "lotus-eat" undisturbed in its sea-girt happy isolation'.

Maldivians are peace-loving and violent crimes like murder and rape are extremely rare. In applying *shari'a*, Maldives' courts are lenient. Fines are imposed for petty crime. Only once in this century, during the reign of Amin Didi, have thieves had their hands amputated. In the old days, murderers were flogged through the streets before being banished to a remote island for life.

Only recently have prisons been established for serious criminals and political detainees. People are still flogged with a *durra*, a taut leather strap with flat copper studs down the sides. Adulterers are not stoned to death, but they do undergo flogging on their thighs. The most common and traditional punishment is house arrest or banishment to an island far away from family and friends.

Those caught drinking alcohol are usually flogged with a *durra* and banished for a year. If a banished person works hard and improves his behaviour, he can become a respected member of the local community. With a new sense of self-esteem, it is extremely rare that he commits a crime again.

The Maldivian character is certainly very different from the toiling, harassed Westerner who has little time for a simple existence in harmony with nature. To many Europeans, Maldivians will no doubt appear relaxed — 'laid-back'. One of the great attractions of Maldives is that in so many ways it seems to offer an exemplary way of life adapted to the environment. What was once decried as apathy and indifference can now be seen as virtue: the art of enjoying a full and contented life without drudgery.

Yet this Western image of Maldivians as 'lotus eaters' in a lost paradise is quite misleading. To scratch a living, the islanders work long, dangerous, and hard hours, mainly fishing. They are entirely dependent on the sea and at the mercy of the elements. Women worry about how to make ends meet, and the men worry about their catch. Most families are split by the need for the men to go away, either to work in the resorts or aboard foreign shipping lines.

There is an element of resignation and stoicism in the Maldivian approach to life. Perhaps because they go away and come back so often, they have no word in *Dhivehi* for 'goodbye' or 'hello'. At the same time, the Maldivian interest in political intrigue and the volatile nature of their personal relations no doubt reflect the need to express emotions that are repressed in the close-knit, all-embracing island communities.

Of course, things are changing in the capital and surrounding islands, where the influence of the outside world is so much greater. Gone are the days when the Maldivians were reliant on the wily merchants of southern India or Sri Lanka for their economy. Now they run their own businesses, and there is a growing number of wealthy entrepreneurs in the country. Government officials only work in the morning and do other jobs in the afternoon.

Although still predominantly an Islamic seafaring nation, Maldives is rapidly adapting to the modern world. In the 1970s, the ornate doors of the country started to creak open as tourists began to discover this 'lost paradise' in the middle of the Indian Ocean.

The trickle has now become a flood. The ancient ways and rhythms of this unique cluster of islands are undergoing profound change as a result of the modern influences from the world outside. At this stage, it is difficult to say what the long-term effects may be. What is certain is that the riddle and the fascination of Maldives will remain for a long time to come.

Inevitably most visitors to Maldives will end up on a resort island, but the only way to really get to know Maldives is by ship. Millionaires on their beautiful schooners can occasionally be seen anchored offshore from the resort islands. Smaller yachts of seasoned enthusiasts also sail through the islands, conscious of the uncharted dangers of the coral reefs.

But the finest way to see the archipelago is by *dhoani*, the traditional wooden Maldivian schooner with a diesel engine and lateen sail, on a real *Journey through Maldives.*

Opposite: Two essential ingredients of life in Maldives — sunlight and coconut palms. Coconut trees supply the islanders with food, shelter, and materials for their boats.

2. *The Pearl in the Necklace*

Tiny Malé Island is one of the smallest capitals in the world — too small even to boast its own airport. The jetliners that bring tourists from all over the world land on the neighbouring island of Hulhule.

Providentially near the capital, this long thin stretch of land serves as a natural aircraft carrier permanently anchored in the sea: it is the only international runway in the world that begins and ends in water. Just as the jumbo jets seem about to splash into the sea, their wheels suddenly bounce onto a strip long enough for them to come to a safe halt.

Now one form of transport is abandoned for another. At the jetty alongside the airport *dhoanis* and launches wait to take the passengers to the capital and the surrounding resort islands. The *dhoanis* have been turned into ferries, but many still have beautifully painted prows curving high in the sky like the boats of the ancient Phoenicians.

The *raison d'être* of the airport is undoubtedly tourism, which is relatively new to Maldives and has brought prosperity to the capital and the necklace of islands around it in Malé Atoll. The first tourists arrived in 1972, under President Nasir, when an Italian operator opened up a resort village on the island of Kurumba (Vihamanaafushi) in Malé Atoll. In Maldives, Europeans discovered a 'lost tropical paradise' reminiscent of the Polynesian islands before they were spoilt by Western contact, but with a unique combination of the sophisticated and the simple.

The resorts evoke the classic Western fantasy of the desert island — multicoloured coral reefs, turquoise lagoons, white coral beaches, luxuriant tropical vegetation, palm trees dipping into the tepid water, and sun, sun, and more sun. These pristine beaches are washed by the waters of the least polluted ocean in the world. For a brief spell, stressed city-dwellers from the north can leave their hectic urban lives and fly into simple naturalness and try to learn the art of doing nothing gracefully; of simply eating, swimming, relaxing, and sleeping, their heads full of sunny seascapes, tropical ebony nights under pin-bright stars, and swaying coconut palms.

A visit to Maldives leaves memories of large images and grand vistas under the infinite fire of the Equatorial sun. Of course, the everyday reality may be a little different.

For a start, you will not be alone and the friendly locals will be speaking your language behind desks and bars. While the setting might be natural and primitive, the luxury and sophistication are imported. The resort islands boast an extraordinary collection of fanciful buildings and an infrastructure based on the most advanced technology — in total contrast to the neighbouring islands where Maldivians, who have adapted so carefully to their maritime environment, continue to live as they have done for centuries. Your barman may drink but more likely than not he is a Buddhist from Sri Lanka. If a Maldivian is caught drinking, they are banished for a year to a remote island to meditate on their transgression of Qur'anic law.

Most resorts cater for groups. It is difficult for the independent traveller to hop from island to island, but not impossible. But any foreigner now has to pay a daily tax while they are in the country and must have a 'sponsor' in order to stay on an inhabited island. On arrival, the visitor must also inform the local island chief (*katheeb*).

To become a Maldives citizen you must be a Muslim. It is also

Previous pages: Only one and a half square kilometres in size, Malé is one of the smallest capitals in the world. Yet as the hub of the atolls, its population has swollen to more than 70,000 — almost one-third of the country's entire population. The area to the right was recently reclaimed from the sea.

Following pages: Malé's inner harbour is enclosed by a coral stone breakwater built in the early seventeenth century. Ocean-going vessels anchor out in the main channel and unload their cargoes into smaller boats which ferry them ashore.

Opposite: Malé International Airport, situated on Hulhule Island, only ten minutes by boat from the capital, serves as a natural aircraft carrier anchored in the sea. It is the only international runway in the world that begins and ends in the water.

necessary to be one to marry a Maldivian. Gone are the days when a passing sailor simply married a girl for a few weeks and then divorced her as he set sail. And it is no longer possible to land on some desert island, build a shack, and live the life of a 'lotus eater'.

All the islands are owned by the government and leased to local and foreign operators. The tourist industry is now the foremost earner of foreign exchange and the most dynamic sector of the economy. In 1991, over 196,000 tourists visited the islands, more than a fourfold increase since 1980, accounting for three-fifths of visible export earnings. Some of the uninhabited islands are earmarked for future development.

Altogether, there are about seventy resort islands, rarely more than a couple of hours from the airport or capital by boat. Each one is quite flat and low lying, with coconut trees towering over the tropical shrubs and flowers, surrounded by a wide strand of dazzling white coral sand. On the bottom of the shallow inner lagoon this turns the water into a brilliant turquoise, but beyond the protective coral reef the sea floor drops hundreds of fathoms into the deep blue of the Indian Ocean. You can explore most islands in less than ten minutes. Some, like the crescent-shaped island of Baros, for instance, are only 500 metres long and 200 metres wide.

Managed by different companies, the resorts usually develop their own styles and standards. Some companies, like the French Club Méditerranée or the Italian Club Vacanze, dovetail their programmes for particular tastes and nationalities.

These islands are entirely self-contained communities. You need not be stranded, however, for visits can be arranged to other resort islands, neighbouring desert islands, or even to some inhabited islands where Maldivians manufacture handicrafts for the visitors. In most cases, European travel companies have tried to recreate the European ideal of tropical island living, combining natural beauty with creature comforts. Maldives supplies the sand, sun, and sea while virtually everything else — from light bulbs, alcohol, and even tropical fruit — is imported.

The resorts vary widely, from the most sophisticated comforts ensconced in post-modernist architecture, to neat and clean villas made from coral and thatch similar to those used by Maldivians. Kurumba, for instance, the first tourist resort opened in Maldives, has a freshwater swimming pool and a fully equipped sports centre with a gym, tennis courts, sauna, jacuzzi, and billiard room. Cocoa is a hideaway where the very rich seek relaxation and seclusion, offering the feeling of a private island for only eight or ten guests.

At the other extreme, the Club Méditerranée or the Italian Club Vacanze offers non-stop fun with such non-Maldivian activities as aerobics, archery, and squash as well as the usual watersports. The Velassaru resort, in which each room has its own garden with one member of staff to every guest, has been rated one of the best hotels in the world.

As the demand for more island hideaways increases, resorts are being built further and further away from Malé and the airport. Indeed, Helegeli lies about fifty kilometres from the airport on the ancient seaway to the northern atolls, while Kuramathi is sixty kilometres west of the airport. The most remote island resort, Kunfunadhoo in Baa Atoll

Above: At Rihiveli Island, tourists discover the joys of crystal-clear waters, azure skies, and sunny Maldivian days by catamaran.

Above: Air Maldives aircraft makes a low pass over one of the islands. The airline provides an inter-island service to a number of islands throughout Maldives.

to the north, takes about two and a half hours to reach by boat. But wherever they may be, all these resort islands boast their own natural beauty, unique ecosystem, and tranquil atmosphere.

The accommodation usually consists of villas with thatched or tiled roofs circling the island near the beach. If you open the windows and turn off the air-conditioning you can hear the sea breeze whispering in the palm trees and the gentle crashing of the surf on the beach. Some islands have beautiful terraces built out into the lagoon from which, in the translucent water below, you can watch the reef fish.

The cultural impact of tourism has been diminished by keeping the tourists on these islands that now appear like so many satellites around the capital. Few Maldivians live permanently on the resort islands, and those that do are nearly all men. There is very little contact between the tourists and locals, except in the tea and tourist shops of Malé. Independent travellers living on a pittance, who came to Maldives in the 1970s looking for desert islands on which to become Robinson Crusoes, have also been discouraged.

Even on the most sophisticated island, the atmosphere is relaxed and

Opposite: Shining in the tropical sun, the beautiful minaret and mosque of Malé's Islamic Centre. A Sunni Muslim society of the liberal Shafi'ite school, every citizen of Maldives must be a Muslim and the law of the land is based on the Islamic code of Shari'a.

Above: Modest Presidential Palace, known as the Muleeaage, originally built in Malé by Sultan Shamsuddeen III for his son just before the First World War. The colonial-style building was turned into the President's home in 1953 when the country became a republic.

informal. Potential tourists are warned: 'Strictly Prohibited — Hurry, Worry, Rush, Rush'. Serenity, tranquillity, and natural harmony are the key words of the tourist brochures, which entice with such slogans as 'Robinson Crusoe with Air-Conditioning' or 'Where French Chic Goes Native'. For those who do not want to feel too disorientated a 'Romantic Island Hideaway with a Mediterranean Atmosphere' is on offer.

To a large extent these clichés are true. A resort island is a place for no news and no shoes, a place to grip hold of the sand with bare feet, and to throw one's body into the sea; to fill the head with vast seascapes, bright stars at night, red orbs of sun falling into the sea; to smell bougainvillaea, frangipani, and hibiscus flowers, and to admire the banyan, bamboo, coconut, and mangrove trees; to look at a heron dipping its long beak as shoals of tiny silver fish splash at the water's edge, or to see a flying fox stretching its wings overhead as it makes for another island; to watch little crabs scuttling away across the sand as you walk home along a moonlit beach.

However, because of the rise in sea-levels from global warming,

Opposite: Imposing entrance of Malé's Islamic Centre. Opened in 1984, it contains a library and conference hall, as well as the principal mosque of the country.

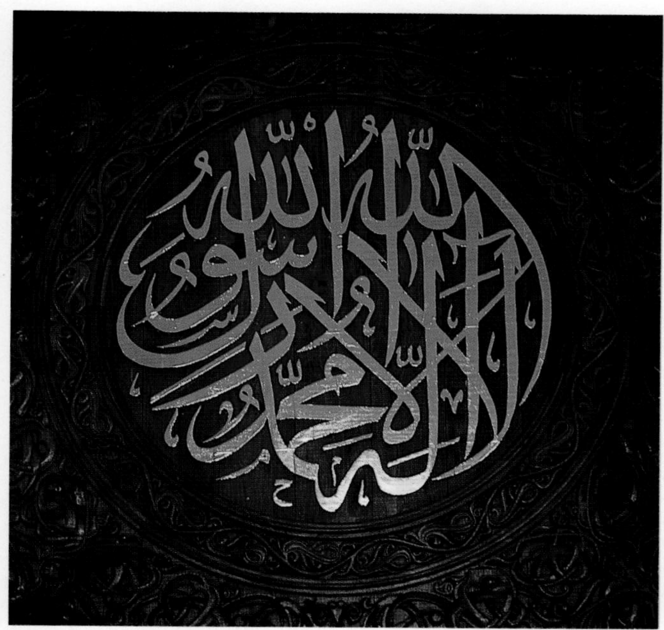

Above: Elegantly carved panel and beautifully designed calligraphy decorate the interior walls of the grand mosque in Malé.

Opposite: Interior of the grand mosque of the Islamic Centre, Malé, where more than 5,000 worshippers gather for Friday prayers. The mihraab *in the middle points in the direction of Mecca, towards which all devout Muslims turn to say their prayers five times a day.*

scientists predict that these magic islands may well be washed away within fifty years. The protective coral reefs may not be able to grow at the same rate as the rise in sea-level, in which case a tidal surge or a storm may sweep across the islands taking all the beautiful vegetation, elegant buildings, and ancient ruins with them. Left over would be a barren spit of coral sand and an occasional interesting diving site.

Tourism has created jobs and provided revenue for schools and health clinics in the outlying atolls. It has also stimulated dying handicrafts such as mat-weaving, lacquerwork, and jewellery. While some crafts, like stone-carving, had already died out, the new demand revived others. Traditional dances too have been resuscitated in order to show tourists something of Maldivian culture.

At the same time, tourism undoubtedly exerts an enormous influence on island life, even in the most remote atolls. Many men, particularly those from the south who learned English at the former British airbase on Gan, are separated from their families for most of the year while working in the resort satellites around Malé. They learn new skills and languages, but are also exposed to a new and strange way of life. When they return home with their Western clothes and new-found wealth, they are conspicuous. If they are young, they tend to invest in a prestigious motorbike.

Traditionally, Maldivians are shy and taciturn with strangers, particularly non-Muslims. With their red faces, shorts, colourful shirts, and inevitable cameras, the tourists landing on Malé's waterfront in search of souvenirs and suntan lotion are very visible. To entice them into shops, Western pop music blares out and all manner of trinkets are on sale. Restaurants with names like Downtown, Quench, and Newport cater for European tastes and pockets. Undoubtedly, the young in Malé are intrigued by these people from far-flung parts of the world.

The new tourist buildings and visitors have wrought profound change on the ecology of the islands. The increase in coral mining around Malé for building materials has weakened the protective reefs. Walking on or touching coral in the water can also kill the tiny polyps which keep the whole reef alive. Leaching of nitrates from waste water has encouraged the growth of weed in some areas. Jetties for boats too have checked the natural swirling movement of the sand around the islands with the tide, causing erosion on one side and silting on the other.

Keen to restore the natural equilibrium, the government is making careful studies of the effects on the environment, fully realizing that the primary attraction of Maldives is that of a relatively unpolluted marine ecosystem.

Early visitors plundered the reefs, but collecting coral and shells and spear fishing with harpoon guns is now forbidden. Even the shark-feeding by skilled local divers that once made Maldives famous is now officially discouraged. The unwelcome circus interferes with the natural behaviour of the sharks. Maldives may be a place where the overfed sharks are friendly, but are the people friendly to the sharks?

Walking along the waterfront of Malé, it is difficult to realize that until recently the country was quite cut off from the rest of the world. Most people who work in the offices in the capital now wear modern dress — men in trousers and short-sleeved shirts and the women in skirts and

blouses. But many men wear a sarong around their waist and women still wear the traditional dress — the long black skirt (*kandiki*) worn under a long-sleeved dress (*libaas*), which fits tightly across the arms and chest and loose around the thighs. The latter is generally made from dark-blueish or brown-coloured material, lined and trimmed with a collar of braid woven from silver, gold, and coloured threads. Some older women still gather their hair into a round, flat chignon on the right side of their head. The pious Ibn Battuta was shocked to see the women topless, but he failed to persuade them to cover themselves. Only about fifty years ago did they begin to hide their breasts.

When Bell stayed in Malé in 1921 he remarked that 'with its teeming population of over 5,200 souls, [it] is far too overcrowded already'. Yet as the hub of the atolls it has grown rapidly since and now has about 60,000 inhabitants — about one-third of the entire population, including a floating population of several thousand people who come to sell their wares and buy goods. To cope with the swelling population land has been reclaimed in the shallow waters

Above: Opening of parliament, the Citizens' Majlis, *a forty-eight member body that includes two representatives from each atoll, two from the capital, and eight presidential appointees.*

inside the southern and western reefs, adding almost one-third again to the island's original size. Still this is not enough.

For centuries Malé has been the political, economic, and cultural centre of Maldives. Although there are no factories or skyscrapers, Malé is the home of all government offices, banks, and communications — and of all the key public and private organizations that oversee the economic and social life of the nation. But while the atolls are mainly dependent on the sea for their livelihood, ultimately Malé is dependent on the atolls for its economic wellbeing. From all over the archipelago, islanders come to do business in the waterfront offices, the 'Singapore bazaar', and the small shops in the narrow lanes where nearly all the goods are imported. The Rufiya is now the common currency, but it is the American dollar which is sought after.

The trading connections that money buys are still as extensive as they were centuries ago. Today it is possible to see men carrying sacks and goods from moored *dhoanis* and piling them up on the waterfront before they are distributed to those who ordered them. A quick glance will show the extent of existing trading connections: rice from Burma; vegetable oil, flour, and biscuits from Singapore (which acts largely as an entrepôt); onions from India, betel nuts from Sri Lanka, detergent from China, sugar from France, and butter from Ireland.

Crossing from the airport to Malé, you soon see the real lifeblood of the nation. The great liners, tankers, and cargo ships that bring all the islands need for building, food, and energy ride high at their moorings in the roadstead. The passing *dhoanis* that forever crisscross to and fro amongst these silent and brooding beasts of the high seas seem like so many little buzzing insects. The expanse of sea that lies between the islands of Funadhoo, Dhoonidhoo, and Viligili where the great ocean-going ships lie at anchor is called the 'outer harbour'. Their cargoes are ferried by towed lighters to the wharfs in the inner harbour, north of the capital.

Malé's inner harbour, enclosed by a coral-stone breakwater with narrow entrances, was first built between 1620 and 1648. Different sections of the waterfront have different functions: one section is for the ferry boats and *dhoanis* to the outlying islands, another for landing fish and local products for the market. A new wooden official jetty is situated in front of the headquarters of the Security Forces.

The most striking building that dominates the skyline in Malé when you approach it from the sea is the shining gold dome and thin minaret of the new Islamic Centre. Opened in 1984, it has a library and conference hall. Its central feature, however, is the grand mosque which can hold more than 5,000 people. It is named after the national hero Sultan Muhammad Thakurufaanu. The Islamic Centre not only emphasizes the Muslim faith of the Maldivians but also reflects the prosperity that has come to the islands.

There are several other monuments to the Islamic past on the island. A memorial called Medhu Ziyaarath commemorates the person who is said to have converted Maldives to Islam in AD 1153 — one Abu al Barakaath Yusuf al Barbari, also referred to as Abdul Rikaab Yoosuful al Thabreyzee.

Opposite is the most beautiful mosque on Malé — the Hukuru Miskiy

Opposite: Illuminated interior of ancient mosque highlights the beautiful wooden carvings and lacquered pillar tops supporting the roof, reflecting the high skills of Maldivian craftsmen.

Above: Gleaming white Munnaaru *(minaret), built in 1675 by Sultan Ibrahim Iskandar, next to the Hukuru Miskiy or Friday Mosque built by the same sultan nineteen years earlier. Before the Islamic Centre opened, the chief* mudhimu *or muezzin of Malé called the faithful to prayer from the minaret. The ornately carved stone exterior of the mosque has been covered with a corrugated iron roof to protect it from the piercing rays of the sun.*

or Friday Mosque. Built in 1656 during the reign of Sultan Ibrahim Iskandar, the interior and exterior walls are intricately carved with Arabic writings and ornamental patterns. The compound encloses a number of ancient tombstones, all beautifully carved, erected to the memory of past sultans and dignitaries.

In 1675, the same sultan also built the nearby *Munnaaru* (minaret), modelled on the minarets he had seen on a pilgrimage to Mecca. Before the Islamic Centre was built, the chief *mudhimu* or muezzin on the island used to call the faithful to prayer from there.

The most remembered episode in Maldives' past is commemorated by the tomb of Muhammad Thakurufaanu. His liberation of Maldives from the Portuguese is celebrated on Maldives' National Day on the first of the month of the *Rabeeu'l Awwal* in the Islamic Calendar. Thakurufaanu, who died in 1585, is also remembered for minting the country's first coins, improving the level of education and religious services, and expanding trade.

Successive rulers have drawn inspiration from Thakurufaanu as a national hero to weld the scattered people of the Maldives into one

Above: Beautifully designed and executed brass plaque with a cut-glass boss reflects the care and skill that went into the smallest detail of Malé's Friday Mosque.

nation. But other buildings in Malé speak of the country's tempestuous political history this century when different parties have schemed, plotted, and fought for the sultanship. The Presidential Palace, known as the Muleeaage, was built just before the First World War to honour Sultan Shamsuddeen III's son. The sultan, however, was deposed soon after and his son never took office. When the country became a republic in 1953, the modest colonial-looking building became the Presidential Palace.

The country reverted to a sultanate after the short-lived republic, but when Maldives became a republic again in 1968 the grand Sultan's Palace was razed to the ground — except for one three-storey building — and the grounds became a public park. Only the massive iron gate at the entrance speaks of its former glory. The building which survived has become the National Museum. The former sultan's gardens have ponds full of water lilies and trees full of singing birds, a quiet green oasis in the now bustling capital.

The National Museum houses an interesting collection of royal possessions, but some of the most interesting exhibits are its archaeological finds. Spread along a verandah and in a small room are the intriguing remains gathered from temples scattered throughout the atolls.

Among the most fascinating artefacts are two five-faced statues recently discovered in Malé. With long feline teeth, outstretched tongues, and extended ear lobes, they look like devils.

Most of the objects in the museum belonged to former sultans: thrones, sedan chairs, ceremonial parasols, palanquins, and a collection of boxes decorated with intricate lacquerwork. The museum houses not only the paraphernalia of sultanship, but also a motorbike with its petrol tank blown out by a bullet — souvenir of the abortive 1988 coup attempt.

Earlier twentieth-century visitors noted how peaceful Malé was with its clean rectangular streets of coral sand and its one-storey coral buildings behind neat palisades. When the Englishwoman Lawson Robins visited the capital in 1920 — one of the few white women seen there in many years — she noted that there was no telegraph, no bullock carts, motors, or carriages. It was 'a land of quietness and peace'.

Some of the best houses have walls of whitewashed coral stones; but most are in a tiny compound surrounded by a fence of cadjan. *Trees and shrubs flourish: we saw firs, oleanders, bamboos, palms and other plants. . . . Each street was carpeted with white coral sand, soft and clean.*

When the English traveller T. W. Hockly visited Malé in 1934, he too recorded:

The roads are all of white coral sand and I have never seen any place kept cleaner. There were several small shops and a few houses where plantain, papaya and mango trees, and many shrubs were flourishing luxuriously. . . . The poorer inhabitants have their houses walled with mats or cadjans *made from palm leaves, about six to seven feet in height. Every little dwelling stands in its own compound. They are roofed with* cadjans *or corrugated iron sheets.*

While this description could still apply to villages in the outlying

Above: In a world without alcohol, dhufaa echchethi *— thin, crispy slices of areca-nut* (foah) *laid out on a piece of betel leaf* (bileh) *— provides a mild stimulant. It is usually chewed with a clove, some lime made from ground coral, and a little tobacco. From about the age of fourteen, most Maldivians chew the concoction. The tightly rolled pieces of newspaper on sale — known as* bidi *— contain dark-brown imported tobacco.*

Above right: Local produce at Malé's fruit and vegetable market. With little arable land available on the islands, vegetables form only a small part of the Maldivian diet. The bottles contain dhiyaa hakuru, *the deliciously sweet syrup tapped from coconut trees which tastes like honey.*

islands, Malé has experienced irrevocable change. Many trees disappeared after the Second World War when Muhammad Amin Didi issued a decree that the main roads in the country should be widened. Building blocks and cement bricks have replaced the *cadjan*. The sand in the streets is grey rather than white. Hard-core roads with pavements crisscross the shopping centre.

Nowadays the island population is so big and land so scarce that the traditional single-storey coral houses are being replaced by modern buildings, although none is usually higher than five storeys and most only two. In every quarter of the island, there are signs of hectic building. New money and new people make them inevitable.

While most houses have names in *Dhivehi*, many have delightful English ones, often quite incongruous and poetic, such as Snow Down, Sky Villa, Rose Burn, Night Flower, Lightning Villa, Dreamy Light, Crab Tree, and Blue Bell. Green and blue seem to be favourite colours.

There are no international hotels in the capital — they are found on the resort islands — but there are some private and government-run guesthouses and small hotels.

Motorbikes, cars, vans, and lorries are beginning to pollute the air and ears — about 2,000 of them. As yet there are no buses but more and more taxis are being unloaded at the wharf. Outside government offices, row upon row of solid Raleigh bicycles show how the pace of life has quickened. It only takes twenty minutes to cross the island on foot, but even this is considered too long. By contrast, in the evening joggers take to the streets to run around the island in order to keep fit. In the rainy season, some streets can be under a foot or more of water.

Walking along the bustling streets of Malé, it is difficult to realize how swiftly the twentieth century has imposed itself on these islands. The modern infrastructure of the nation was not laid down until the 1970s and the first commercial jet did not land until 1977. In the same year a satellite earth station made international telecommunications possible. Colour television was introduced the following year. Since then, Malé has never looked back.

Though it sits in an ocean, water is a problem throughout Maldives. The traditional water supply on the islands is a well dug into the sand: the water that filters through the sand is drinkable but sometimes salty. While Maldivians like this water to wash in, foreigners usually hanker after hot freshwater showers to wash away the sand and salt of the day.

To overcome the problem, desalination plants have been introduced and every effort made to store rainwater from roofs, but on some islands only brackish water is available for washing.

In the western quarter of Malé, you may encounter some of the Giraavaru people who were moved from the neighbouring island of Giraavaru to Hulhule due to erosion of their island. When the airport in Hulhule was extended, they were then moved to Malé, where living conditions were better. They claim to be the original inhabitants of Maldives, and throughout the centuries have kept themselves apart from the rest of society. They are generally considered descendants of Tamils from southern India.

The women are recognizable by their custom of tying their hair in a bun on the right-hand side of their head (other Maldivians tie it on the left). They also have a special kind of silver embroidery around the top of their *libaas* dress. The women are extremely modest; it is said that they do not completely undress themselves, even in front of their husbands.

The Giraavaru not only have different customs but speak with a different accent than other people on Malé, in a way closer to the dialect of Seenu Atoll (Addu Atoll) in the south. Tragically, they will not be around for long. Their numbers are reduced to about 150. As the young are now marrying outside their group and trying to make it in mainstream society, it is unlikely that they will remain an identifiable people for more than a generation. They will become yet another unique community obliterated by the forces of modernity.

Malé is almost the geographical centre of the archipelago, with communication lines fanning out to the outlying atolls, and the administrative, commercial, and political centre. Like the sultans and their officials before, the President and civil servants direct and control all external trade and internal commerce. Malé also contains the greatest wealth in the country and is the centre of justice and religion.

Not surprisingly, like many capitals in the developing world, Malé is a magnet that draws the young. People from other islands go there for special medical attention. In addition, nearly all secondary government and private schools are in Malé, except for one government secondary school recently opened in the southernmost Addu Atoll. Even though the modern education system has been introduced to the atolls,

Above: Old etched brass plaque with flowing Arabic characters on the finely carved tombstone. As Islam took deeper root in the country during the middle ages, the influence of Arabic on the educated classes increased.

Above: Tombstones of famous dignitaries of both sexes in the cemetery of the Friday Mosque in Malé. The large buildings contain the remains of past sultans.

traditional private schools (*makthab*) which teach pupils to understand the rudiments of the Qur'an and to read and write in the mother tongue of *Dhivehi* play a vital role. Only in Malé are there further education institutes. Since graduates are bound to work for the government for two years, they tend to stay in the capital. Afterwards few wish to return to the outlying atolls. There is no problem in finding a job in Malé. Life, too, is more exciting, with cinemas showing Hindi romances and epics and local television broadcasting every night. Whereas the traditional island community is close-knit and all-encompassing, the anonymity of the town enables the young to be more independent from their families and lead their own lives.

For the average Maldivian, it is the gateway to almost every opportunity in life. Indeed, the political history of Maldives is largely the history of the major families on Malé.

Although Maldivian society does not have a strict caste system as in India, there are important social divisions. The upper class were close friends and relatives of the sultan and his family with names like Kalo, Fulu, Maniku, and Didi. Even among these families there were important

Above: Surrealistic jaws of sharks in a tourist shop in Malé, with the midday sun reflecting the street life — and the photographer's camera — in the shop window.

divisions. Well into this century, H.C.P. Bell noted that 'a Didi marrying a Maniku lady raises her to his own rank; but the children of a Maniku father and Didi mother are, strictly speaking, not entitled to the appellation Didi'. In the past it was considered unacceptable to eat with a member of an inferior class, or for an inferior person to sit with a superior except on a low stool. Nowadays these distinctions are breaking down, and sometimes Maniku and Didi are even used as nicknames.

Today advancement is based more on merit than birth, although education is now less important than wealth to command respect from others. The number of islands a person leases or the number of boats he owns remains crucial to social standing.

The boat owner takes about half the day's catch, while the skipper (*keyolhu*) earns about one-fifth. The rest is divided equally among the fishermen. The men who make the boats (*maavadin*) are highly respected craftsmen; on their skill depends the fishermen's lives and the well-being of the community. On the same social rung are the medicine men (*hakeems*). Skilled traders like blacksmiths and jewellers also command respect. At the bottom of the social rung is the toddy-tapper (*raiveri*) who

Above: After a hard day's work in the merciless sun the youngest member of the crew of a fishing dhoani *jumps happily ashore as the vessel arrives at Malé's inner harbour in the late afternoon.*

gathers the honey, looks after the coconuts, and taps the sap for toddy.

Although in its early history Maldives was ruled by sultanas and may have had a matrilineal system of inheritance, it tends today to be a man's world. Traditionally, men used to eat before the rest of the family. However, this is less common in today's society — although most major decisions are still made by the men, while the women are expected to stay at home and look after the family. Today, this is not always the case. Couples marry at an extremely early age, between the ages of fifteen and sixteen, but with the highest divorce rate in the world, there is little fuss. The ceremony takes place either in the groom's house or the island chief's office without the bride. It is enough for the groom, his father, the uncle of the bride, and two witnesses to go to the local judge (*gazi*) to formalize it.

Under Islamic law, men are allowed to take four wives — and in the past it was considered a mark of esteem and piety to have so many. Today Maldivian men rarely marry more than one wife. Although some marriages are still arranged, there is an increasing desire for romantic love, partly inspired by Hindi romantic films and Western literature.

Above: Day's catch of skipjack tuna — kandu mas *— laid out before being passed ashore to the fish market on Malé's waterfront. Fishing* dhoanis *leave the islands in search of tuna, which they still catch by the traditional pole-and-line method, early in the morning. On an exceptionally good day, up to 1,000 fish can be caught.*

It is even easier to divorce. The husband merely has to say *thalaaq* ('I divorce you') — and then report the fact to the judge.

For the woman, divorce is more difficult. She must take her case to the judge and prove cruelty, desertion, or adultery. There are strong Muslim sanctions against adultery, however, and culprits are flogged. Therefore many couples form temporary liaisons within the marriage tie, in some cases for just a few weeks. One well-placed citizen of Malé is reputed to have married eighty-six times. Ten times is not uncommon but the average is four marriages in a lifetime. Eight out of ten people divorce at least once. Most marriages are between people from the same island. No doubt the suspicion and drama involved in such a high divorce rate alleviate the monotony of island life.

Some newly married couples arrange a *kaiveni sai,* a small reception with tea and snacks and perhaps some dancing. Grander affairs, however, are being introduced. Daughters of wealthy families on Malé celebrate in style with up to 250 guests.

On such occasions the trees are often decorated with tinsel and coloured paper; if electricity has arrived on an island in the shape of a

Following pages: Crew row their becalmed dhoani *through the narrow channel of a reef entrance marked by an old, weather-beaten branch.*

Above: Modern sun-worshippers enjoy the peace and beauty of Maldives under the Equatorial sun.

generator, the whole compound may be lit with fairy lights.

Despite the high divorce rate children suffer few problems. The close-knit island communities practice mutual aid to survive difficult circumstances. Extended families look after their own members, and it is often the mother's family that looks after the children of a divorced couple.

Few families say a great deal or express emotions strongly. Indeed, it is extremely rare to hear anyone raise their voice, even to children, many of whom rarely speak to their remote if respected fathers.

Husbands provide the facilities and money for the two meals that most families enjoy each day. Women also earn extra cash from mat weaving or coir making.

Since many men are usually away working, women are responsible for the everyday running of the home. Their greatest problems are concerned with the education of the children, buying enough food, and worrying about the fishing. On some islands, you will rarely see a man between the age of eighteen and forty-five.

Under the present constitution, the President is considered the religious and political leader of the country. Nowadays, under the

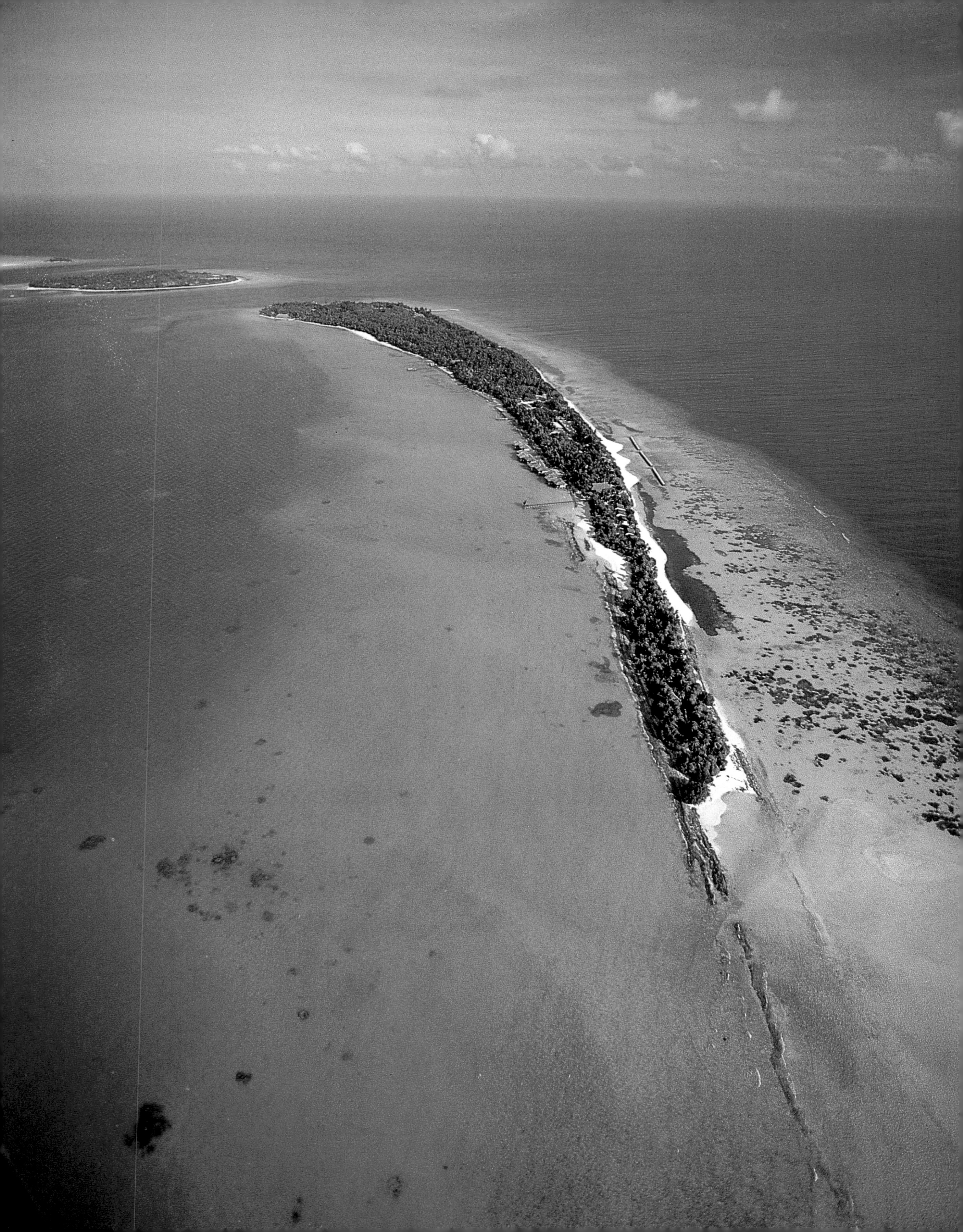

Above: Resort island in Malé Atoll where hard-pressed visitors try to learn the art of doing nothing gracefully.

Right: On Gangehi Island, over-water bungalows, pyramids made from palm thatch, gleaming white coral beaches, and warm, crystal-clear water — all part of the unique experience of holidaying in Maldives.

Left: Curving beauty of Kuramathi Island on the outer rim of Alifu Atoll where the coral reef drops precipitously down into the deep blue for more than 1,000 fathoms. The English word 'atoll' comes from the Dhivehi *word* atholhu.

Opposite: Well-laden dhoani, *the lifeline between the far-flung islands of Maldives. While still carrying their traditional lateen sails, most* dhoanis *now rely on diesel engines to ply their routes. In the background is one of the ferry* dhoanis *that trade between the islands.*

Above: Amphibious microlight plane, with a rubber dinghy hull, soars above the palms for a bird's-eye view of the watery world of Maldives.

Opposite: Transport ancient and modern. The sea is no longer the only means of travelling between the far-flung islands of the Maldivian archipelago.

Islamic law of *shari'a,* men deal with religious and judicial affairs. No woman can be a judge. Women say different prayers and have their own mosques. Indeed, in the 1940s and 1950s women were allowed to wear only two kinds of dress. Although traditionally Maldivian women never wore *purdah,* the new wave of religious fervour sweeping the Islamic world means that more and more women and girls cover their heads, legs, and arms — a practice called *burugaa* in Dhivehi.

While there are marked differences between rich and poor, especially in Malé, there is no dire poverty. The island community and the extended family act as a safety net for its members. Even in the capital, no one sleeps in the streets or goes to bed hungry. In this sense, being small has its blessings, for everyone knows each other and is willing to lend a hand. Almsgiving is one of the fundamental tenets of Islam.

The economic importance of Malé is obvious in its markets north of the town centre. From about three o'clock in the afternoon fishing *dhoanis* begin to sail into the harbour laden with the day's catch. At sea before dawn, the crews have spent the day under the remorseless tropical sun and the strain shows on their faces. They carry their catch — mainly

Below: Shipshape and Bristol fashion, a schooner lies at anchor on the lee shore of Bandos Island after a day's exhilarating sailing in the waters around Malé Atoll.

Opposite: Aboard a diesel-powered fishing dhoani, *fishermen enjoy the tranquillity of the late afternoon under the shade of its auxiliary lateen sail.*

Opposite: Fishing dhoani *in full sail. Traditionally sails were square and made from thatched palm leaves, although the common lateen sail is now woven from cotton strips. The* dhoani *has the same sleek lines as its cousin, the Arabian dhow.*

Below: Guiding the helmsman through the treacherous reefs of the shallow basin within an atoll. Subtle changes in the colour of the sea indicate the varying degrees of depth. The garb of the sailor and the vessel may be new, but the method of navigation is thousands of years old.

Opposite: Coconut roots washed by the warm Indian Ocean on the eroded beach of Bandos Island. The shallow lagoon of white coral sand gives way to a reef which suddenly drops thousands of metres into the deep blue.

Above: All the imported sophistication of the luxury resort islands ensures that wealthy northerners enjoy their touch of the tropical sun in total comfort.

bonito, swordfish, and tuna — ashore where they are laid out for sale in the shade of the market.

The fish market is strictly men's business — the customers are all males, carefully choosing the right fish for their family. The sight of a woman in this inner sanctum raises eyebrows, and only a few women on Malé have witnessed this rite which takes place every afternoon as the sun begins to sink. Indeed, some women are so housebound that they have never walked around the whole island.

The men also do the shopping in the neighbouring wood market, choosing the best bundle of firewood for cooking. The wood — coconut and screwpine as well as *dhakadhaa*, *uni*, and *dhiggaa* — is collected from the surrounding islands and brought in by *dhoani*. On Malé, virtually the only trees left are ornamental coconuts, although some new saplings have been planted on the reclaimed land in the west.

In the same area as the fish and wood markets a covered market with individual stands sells basic commodities for each Maldivian household: rice, coconuts, eggs, oil, spices, sweet potatoes, onions, chillies, watermelons, mangoes, bananas, papaya, pomegranates, limes, vinegar made from coconut sap, and honey. Vegetables are rare and expensive since the islands have such limited arable land. Once the food is brought home by the men, it enters the inner sanctum of the women — the kitchen — where no man sets foot.

As well as the economic and political centre of the country, Malé is also the hub of Malé Atoll, comprising the old North and South Malé atolls. In this double chain of islands that stretches more than 100 kilometres from north to south only ten islands, apart from Malé, are inhabited by islanders. The rest are resort islands for tourists.

Some are reserved for special purposes: Funadhoo, for example, is for the workers who look after the oil tanks there. When Maldives was a British Protectorate, the island of Dhoonidhoo, just north of Malé, boasted the residence of the British representative. The neighbouring island of Kuda Bandos has a happy atmosphere, for on Fridays (the weekly day of prayer and rest) locals from the capital go there to enjoy its delightful beach and lagoon or relax in the shade of its luxuriant vegetation. On other days, anyone can visit it as long as they do not give in to the temptation to stay overnight.

Around Malé, the people of about a dozen islands that were once fishing villages now reap a cash harvest from visiting tourists for whom they make souvenirs and sell handicrafts made elsewhere in the archipelago. Himmafushi and Huraa are both in this category. Others, such as Thulusdhoo, which is ringed by sandy coves, are more traditional. It has warehouses to receive salt fish from fishermen who bring it from northern atolls. Dhiffushi is another fishing island. Other islands are renowned for different things: Gaafaru for one of the largest reefs in Maldives, ten kilometres long and eight kilometres wide, which has proved the undoing of dozens of ocean-going ships; Kaashidhoo, isolated in the northern channel, for its coconut syrup; and Maafushi, for its reformatory school for orphans and delinquents.

*Above: Betwixt sand and foam, the Maldivian little heron (*Butorides striatus didii*) fishes for small fry on the foreshore of a desert island. Considered unique to Maldives, this heron is rarely seen.*

To the west of Malé Atoll, across the forty-kilometre-wide Alihuras channel, stretches Alifu Atoll. Out on its own in the north, a large island called Thoddoo is renowned not only for its watermelon, but for its female dancers who perform the *bandiyaa jehun* by tapping out a rhythm on metal pots.

The island has the remains of a Buddhist temple which, until recently, had a two-metre dome of a small *stupa*. In 1958, a large and complete Buddha was found hidden in a chamber, along with a relic casket containing a silver bowl, a small gold cylinder, and two coins. One coin has been identified from a photograph as a denarius of Caius Vibius Pansa, minted in Rome in 90 BC, a time when the Romans were sailing to Sri Lanka (and therefore through the Maldive islands). The magnificent head of the stone Buddha which was found in the temple is now in the National Museum in Malé.

Tourists generally land at the airport and go straight to the resort of their choice where they can laze on the beach, soak up the sun, or go for a dip in the Indian Ocean. For the more active, a whole range of watersports is available, from windsurfing, canoeing, snorkeling, and scuba diving to water-skiing, parasailing, and fishing. Few will argue with Maldives' claim to offer some of the best diving in the world. The crystal-clear water, the beauty of the coral reefs, and the variety of the marine life are virtually unequalled.

Although visitors usually go to Maldives to get away from it all, in

*Above: Common large grey heron (*Ardea cinerea rectirostris*) in full flight. As many as thirteen different types of heron live in Maldives.*

the high season from November to March the islands often feel crowded. Nevertheless, would-be Robinson Crusoes can usually find a quiet spot all their own or arrange a trip to a neighbouring desert island. Some resorts have their own castaway islands. Rihiveli, meaning 'Silver Sand', has three adjoining uninhabited islands, which can be reached by wading through the shallow lagoon.

On the bigger and more populated islands, it is easy to become addicted to this easy-going, isolated life style. Many diving instructors who have lived on the same island for years say they have never experienced claustrophobia, and many claim that these islands are what they have been looking for all their life.

There are regular sailings from Malé to the outlying atolls by cargo vessels which are usually packed with local passengers and their produce. Conditions are spartan, and you have to be prepared to sleep on deck with others. For those who appreciate a minimum of comfort and a lot of independence then specially adapted 'safari' *dhoanis* are undoubtedly the best. These traditional wooden Maldivian *dhoanis*, with

Opposite: Sundown on the Equator.

Above: Stranded trawler awaits repair. When such a large vessel is pulled ashore, the whole village, including boys and girls, turns out to lend a hand to the ropes.

a diesel engine and lateen sail, have been fitted out with cabins and basic facilities.

They can be a little cramped and short on shower water, and it helps to have sea legs. But the benefits far outweigh the disadvantages. The food is usually more adventurous and Maldivian than in the resorts and the experienced crew of three or four are invariably friendly and accommodating. The overwhelming advantage of such boats is the freedom they offer. With a knowledgeable skipper who knows most of the atolls like the back of his hand, you can get out of the resort satellites around Malé and make for the open sea and islands new.

3. *Emeralds across the Equator*

Separated from the rest of the archipelago by an eighty-five-kilometre stretch of sea known as the One-and-Half-Degree Channel, the southern atolls of Maldives are quite different from those of the north. Three of them vary greatly in size and character: Seenu Atoll, formed like a crescent; Gnaviyani Atoll (Fua Mulaka Atoll), filled in the middle to make one complete island; and the largest atoll in the world, Huvadhoo Atoll, which for administrative purposes has been split into Gaafu Dhaalu and Gaafu Alifu. The names bewilder the visitor, not only because they are often spelt differently, but also because the same atoll usually has several names.

Stretching across the Equator, these remote emerald isles have some of the most fascinating archaeological sites in Maldives. Since they are strategically placed on either side of the Equatorial Channel, the main sea route around southern India, during the centuries they have also received the greatest impact from mariners crisscrossing the Indian Ocean.

Indeed, it made more geographical sense for the southern atolls to trade directly with Sri Lanka than with their own northern neighbours. Colombo is the same distance from them as Malé. Until fairly recently, large sailing ships called *odi*, loaded with dried fish, sailed with the south-west monsoon to Sri Lanka, returning about three months later on the north-east monsoon. Even today it takes two or three days for a cargo vessel to reach Malé. Because of their isolation from the rest of the country, the dialect is so different that people from Malé can understand southerners only with difficulty.

The southern atolls are also widely separated from each other as well as from the north. Each atoll is isolated and largely self-sufficient, and as a result even the dialects and vocabularies change from one atoll to another. If possible, when a person from one atoll visits another he uses the Malé dialect as the common language for communication.

Situated on the southernmost island of Maldives, the airbase on Gan Island in Seenu Atoll has played an important part in the recent history of the south. During the Second World War, when Maldives was still a protectorate, the British navy built an airstrip there. Its strategic importance lay in the fact that all ships navigating around southern Asia had to pass through the Equatorial Channel.

When the British closed their airbase in Ceylon in 1956, they built a new one at Gan. The local inhabitants were simply transferred to the neighbouring island of Feydhoo. Lying 720 kilometres north of the American base on Diego Garcia, it remained in use until 1976 when the British government decided to pull out all its forces east of Suez. Ever since, the superpowers have been interested in leasing the island. For good reason — it contains almost 3,000 metres of runway capable of handling the most advanced jets as well as hangars, permanent barracks, fuel storage tanks, and a pier. Amenities include tennis courts, a football pitch, an overgrown eighteen-hole golf course, and a disused swimming pool. The mosque built by the Pakistani labourers who constructed the runway still stands.

The nonaligned Maldivian government wants to preserve the Indian Ocean as a zone of peace, and so Gan Island remains a semi-

Previous pages: The coral islands of Maldives are thought to have formed millions of years ago when volcanoes emerged from the sea and coral reefs began to grow around their edges. When the volcanic land gradually sank back into the sea, the coral reefs remained. The Maldivian archipelago now forms part of the vast submarine mountain range that stretches across the Indian Ocean from the Lakshadweep Islands in the north to the Chagos Islands in the south.

Opposite: Coconut palms on Fua Mulaku Island hungrily seek the sun, leaning out to sea, as old men and boys wade the shallows in search of reef fish for tuna bait.

Following pages: Two jetties lead to the ideal holiday hideaway where immaculate, air-conditioned bungalows rim this tiny island of tropical perfection.

deserted piece of valuable real estate, where the gardens and lawns are still tended and the roses, bougainvillea, frangipani, and flamboyant trees introduced by the British flourish. Flanked by cannon, a monument commemorating the Indians who died during the Second World War is in good repair. Another legacy that remains is Hammond Innes' 1965 tale *The Strode Venturer*, which was set in Gan. Unfortunately, a recent attempt to create a tourist centre — 'Gan Holiday Village' — in the former sergeant's mess has not succeeded, mainly due to transport difficulties.

Suddenly appearing out of the sky with incredible machines and ideas, the members of the Royal Air Force must have appeared like people from another planet, but they left a good impression. The British legacy remains strong in Seenu Atoll. At its height, the RAF employed some 1,200 workers. The islanders who found employment at the base also benefited from schools and health services. Many of those who learned English are now employed in the tourist resorts in the north.

It was the British who built the causeways connecting the string of islands on the south-west side of the atoll — Feydhoo, Maradhoo, and Hithadhoo — making it possible to travel nine kilometres by road from Hithadhoo to Gan on the longest stretch of road in the whole country and the only road system outside Malé. Unfortunately, the causeways affected the natural flow of the water and the subsequent silting and weed destroyed the once-fine beaches — all to little purpose since most people still travel from one island to the other by boat.

Another unfortunate side effect was that the airbase swept away mysterious archaeological ruins. In 1922, the archaeologist H. C. P. Bell came across a colossal mound about nine metres high with a base measuring eighty square metres 'buried in heavy scrub jungle, interspersed freely with closely growing trees'. Finding a casing of cut coral blocks he concluded that it must have once been a Buddhist *stupa*. Now, cleared by bulldozers, the area has been flattened. The ruin of an old fort which Bell recorded in the northern extremity of the neighbouring island of Hithadhoo has also disappeared. Both must have been important landmarks for mariners rounding the southern tip of Asia.

When you ask who built these mounds, the islanders shrug their shoulders and declare: 'The Redin. Maldivian people could not have built them.' Who the Redin exactly were remains a profound mystery — the stuff of legends. Who knows, perhaps the 'Arif' — the local name for the British Royal Air Force (RAF) — may one day be the legendary but unknown builders in the myths of survivors living in a post-nuclear era!

To develop Gan, and strengthen the ties between north and south, the Malé government set up the Addu Development Authority, which so far has attracted one Hong Kong company which established a garment factory, the only factory. Perhaps not surprisingly, however, the islanders have little interest in the work ethic.

One-third of the 1,200-women work force is from Sri Lanka. The

Above: Children at a traditional makthab *school, where they learn to read and write* Dhivehi *and Arabic and do simple arithmetic.*

Above: Hard-working mother relaxes on a joali, *with her water-cooled hookah or hubble-bubble in which imported tobacco is mixed with syrup drawn from the sap of coconut trees.*

women, who sign one- or two-year contracts, live in the old RAF barracks. Maldivians, who prefer to stay at home, work only periodically — when they need extras or luxuries. If they do not feel like working, they simply stay away. Questioned about the exploitation of local labour, an exasperated manager replied: 'There's no labour to exploit.' Island attitudes take time to change and these independent fisherfolk have little enthusiasm for paid factory work.

Hithadhoo, the most northerly island, is the capital of Seenu Atoll, but only a pilot or someone with local knowledge can reach the island through the coral reefs of the atoll. So shallow is the surrounding water that visiting *dhoanis* have to anchor off a long jetty made from coral blocks where the stinking remains of gutted fish wait for the tide to carry them and their stench away.

Hithadhoo, known as the 'second city' of Maldives, has a population of 10,000. It contains little less than half the total population of the atoll. Its wide, central road, almost like an airstrip, is covered in coral sand and there the pedestrian and the bicycle rule. In the whole atoll there are only twenty taxis and most of them are

Opposite: In a family compound surrounded by coral walls on a southern island, a woman weaves a mat on an ancient hand loom, using locally grown reeds prepared by her friends.

Above: One of two large freshwater lakes on the island of Fua Mulaku (Gnaviyani Atoll) in the south. Several kinds of fish thrive in their warm waters and frogs bellow in the surrounding swamps.

based in Hithadhoo, although an occasional motorbike or pick-up scatters the chickens and brings mothers rushing to collect their offspring playing in the sand.

The town forms a grid pattern with the lanes at right angles to each other. Increasingly, the houses are roofed with corrugated iron rather than coconut thatch and breeze blocks are replacing the small, coral-stone walls. The compounds of most houses are surrounded by walls for privacy. Banana, coconut, and betel nut palms, frangipani and hibiscus flowers flourish in the walled compounds, adding a splash of brilliant colour. Roses, beloved by the British, have also taken root in many gardens.

In the evenings young men play football in the main square opposite the mosque. At the side of the square, girls play a game of *bashi*, in which one player hits a ball over her shoulder with a tennis racket without looking and tries not to be caught out by the eleven members of the opposing team. Loud applause greets every deft move.

The new regional hospital, a government school, and a vocational

Opposite: Intricate and symmetrical Islamic design of a thundu kunaa*, a two-metre mat. It is woven from dried reeds which are dyed naturally with hues of cream, brown, and black.*

centre reflect the government commitment to bring services to the atoll. And one local businessman who succeeded in Malé recently opened an Islamic centre. With so many men working away in the northern tourist resorts, fewer and fewer engage in fishing. Those that do fish sell their catch either to the local market or to the government freezer ship stationed in the area during the fishing season. There is a growing prosperity in the atoll which is reflected in the many half-built houses; sections are added as more money comes in.

Opposite Hithadhoo, on the other horn of the crescent that makes up Seenu Atoll, is the island of Meedhoo. It too has a long coral-rag jetty on its shallow foreshore, where at the first footfall crabs scuttle into their holes. In this town with a population of 2,000 the vegetation is more luxuriant than in the atoll capital and flying foxes crash through the jungle canopy high above, their dark shadows momentarily cutting out the sun's glare. Beautiful fairy terns, known as fair bird (*dhondhooni*), fill the air. Islanders say that because of them there are no crows in Seenu Atoll since they mob any dark birds which may fly in.

Meedhoo is typical of all Maldivian villages. Invariably, there is a wide central road (*magu*) running from one side of the island to the other, while another road crosses it in the middle. At right angles off these main roads run side lanes. The central road usually opens out at the landing point on the beach.

The government, the sole landowner, gives each family an area measuring fifteen by thirty metres, known as a *goathi*, on which to build a homestead. No one is allowed to enter without the family's permission. Inside each compound such trees as papaya and breadfruit, and coconut, areca-nut, and banana palms cast their shade over the colourful gardens. The betel tree, which grows like a vine, is often trained up areca-nut palms. Swinging from the trees are hammock-like chairs (*joali*), which can also be stretched between a wooden frame, and perhaps a wooden, swinging bed (*undhoali*) or two — ideal for relaxation.

The main house in the centre of the compound is used for sleeping and has several rooms. Cooking is done in a separate kitchen (*badige*), usually a coral shack with a thatched roof but no windows, that contains two or three hollows for stoves. Most families have their own well from which they scoop water by means of a large tin can tied to the end of a long thin pole.

Behind an inner enclosure the bathroom (*gifili*) also has a latrine pit dug in the coral sand. ('Going to the beach' does not have the same connotation for a Maldivian as it does for a European. When nature calls many islanders also go down to the seashore, so beware of walking at the water's edge on inhabited islands before the incoming tide has cleared all away.)

Originally, the rectangular houses were built from *cadjan*, but more commonly now walls are made from coral fragments held together with lime which is produced by burning coral slowly for a long time. The coral is mined on the adjoining reefs to a depth of a metre or so. An even stronger 'concrete' can be made by mixing ash and charcoal with the lime along with syrup made from coconut sap.

Above: Surrounded by young green coconuts or kurunba, *this young islander no doubt anticipates the cool, refreshing taste of its delicious milk.*

Above: Young Maldivian girls enjoy a game of bashi *in the village square of Hithadhoo Island. In this uniquely local sport — a cross between tennis and rounders — girls hit a ball over their shoulder with a tennis racket and try not to be caught.*

Islanders today prefer corrugated iron roofs to thatch — although they are much hotter — because they do not have to be replaced every few years. Traditionally, the houses were very dark inside for the windows were small and not intended for cross ventilation. The flat wooden benches that served as beds at night were used as seats during the day. Invariably, a hammock occupied by sleeping babies or the man of the house swung from the rafters. Most of the family's valuables were kept in a trunk under a bed.

Much of the day is spent in the shade of the verandah or under spreading breadfruit or mango trees. Swings and hammocks are favourite lounging spots for grandparents and children. At night, many islanders shut their doors and burn a small kerosene lamp, as in most of the islands electricity is not generated for a full twenty-four hours.

Mothers are busy running the household during the day, tending fires made from scarce wood in smoky kitchens, making the morning's unleavened bread (*roshi*), and preparing rice and fish broth (*garudia*) for the main evening meal. Making the golden syrup (*dhiyaa*

hakuru) from toddy tapped from coconuts involves several hours constant stirring, as does the fish paste (*rihaakuru*) that goes with most meals. Then there are coconuts to grate for curries and to boil for oil. Curing the rock-hard black fillets of tuna (*hiki mas*) takes days.

This basic diet of rice and fish broth, usually enlivened by a spicy side dish of onion and lime (*asaara*), is supplemented between meals by delicious snacks, savouries, and sweets. These include fish balls (*gulha*) and spicy fish and rice cake (*kulhi boakibaa*), or sugary rice balls (*ussakuru gulha*), rice custard (*bondi-baiy*), and gelatin-like cake (*foni boakibaa*), best washed down with the national drink, hot sweet tea (*sai*). For reasons that soon become obvious, Maldivians always eat with the right hand, and hold cutlery or crockery during the meal with the left hand.

The time for relaxation and gossip is when the women sit on their verandahs or in their compounds cleaning the evening's rice, which is spread out on a tray. Young girls collect water from the well in a metal pot which they carry home on their head.

All the womenfolk join in cleaning the compound and the road or

Above: Field of ala *or taro in the freshwater swamps of Fua Mulaku where this root crop grows so well that it has replaced rice as the staple food. One of the most fertile and luxuriant islands in Maldives, Fua Mulaku produces a wide variety of fruit.*

Above: Soon to follow in his father's footsteps, a boy grapples with a harpoon and the classic Maldivian bicycle — a Raleigh.

path outside it, carefully picking up all the leaves and spreading the coral sand evenly with a hand broom (*iloshi fathi*) made from the thin, flexible spines of hundreds of coconut leaves. Occasionally, fresh coral sand is brought from the beach to restore the surroundings to their normal cleanliness.

Shopping, however, is not a major chore, for it is only necessary to walk to the local village store (*fihaara*), which stocks basic items such as rice, sugar, onions, as well as a few luxuries like condensed milk, sweets, oil, and soap.

Unlike their sisters on other Indian Ocean islands, Maldivian women do not market the fish caught by their husbands, but tend the crops and practice handicrafts. To earn a little extra money many women make coir rope from the fibres taken from the husks of coconuts. By threading dried palm leaves together with the coir, they also make *cadjan* for screens and walls. They weave beautiful and intricate mats, showing the same skill in developing abstract patterns as their husbands who build boats simply by using their eye for line and measure. The mat (*saanthi*), woven from thin strips of dried screwpine, is used to sleep on.

The men of Meedhoo used to sell dried fish to Sri Lanka, but now many of them serve on shipping lines or work in the resort islands, remaining away for as long as ten months or a year. This shortage of manpower has clearly affected the local economy, especially the building industry. When the men are away responsibility for the family falls on the women. But these extended families are so used to separation they make little fuss about the coming and going of their menfolk.

Meedhoo boasts that it has sent at least eight judges, the chief interpreters of the Qur'anic law, to Malé. Seven mosques stand on the island and the graves in the old cemetery called Koagannu are still revered. Many have beautifully carved headstones — rounded ones denoting women and ones with a short stub for men — with calligraphic inscriptions. One grave, over 500 years old, contains the remains of Mohamed Shamsuddeen, a famous judge.

Most inscriptions are on greyish coral stone but the more illustrious are burnished with gold leaf. Although the names are written in Arabic, the rest of the inscriptions are in the ancient *Dhivehi* script, *Dhives Akuru*, which dates back 600 years and resembles Sinhala. They are carved so well that they look as if they have been written with pen and ink. Sadly, many of the beautiful tombstones have been broken and the ability to carve such intricate and delicate patterns has long been lost. Indeed, now only a few learned old men remain who are capable of reading these old scripts.

Island hospitality is legendary. Visitors, usually escorted by a swarm of children and at least one upright citizen, are welcomed in the compound of the island chief, where they perch on a hammock (*joali*) under a tree — or on a wooden swingbed (*undhoali*) in his cool and dark house — as he tries to deal with their requests. Guests are served delicious green coconut juice or some other drink, and it is usual to pass round a tray with all the ingredients needed to make a *dhufaa echchethi* — thin, crispy slices of areca-nut, cloves, tobacco, and

lime, wrapped in betel leaf. Together they make a crunchy bite, taken anytime of day and especially after a meal.

The areca-nuts, which are like nutmeg, are sliced very thin and chewed with part of a betel leaf, a little 'lime' (made from ground coral), a clove head, and sometimes some strong moist tobacco kept in a little pot. The imported Indian nuts, drier and more brittle, are generally preferred to the local variety.

Passing the little tray around with all the ingredients on it is one of the first and most important gestures of hospitality to a visitor. Ibn Battuta, who was something of an expert — an addict, in fact — wrote that:

They sweeten the breath and aid digestion, prevent the disagreeable effects of drinking water on an empty stomach, and stimulate the faculties.

Both men and women chew this any time of the day, particularly after meals.

Although there was an attempt in the 1950s to ban smoking as well as alcohol it did not catch on. More often than not, however, the

Above: Well-built mosque from the dressed stone of an earlier pre-Islamic temple near the tomb of the man who brought Islam to the southern atolls. Unfortunately, many of the beautifully carved old tombstones on Fua Mulaku Island have been broken over the years.

Following pages: Boys fishing in the surf off Fua Mulaku for reef fish to be used as bait. Their fathers keep the fish alive in water in the bottom of their boats before throwing them overboard to attract shoals of tuna that are caught by pole and line.

Above: Thatched roof of Kedeyre Mosque by the beach on Fua Mulaku, surrounded by beautifully carved tombstones. The local mudhimu *(muezzin) keeps the mosque immaculately clean and regularly renews the thatched roof. In every village there is at least one mosque for men and another for women.*

women prefer to smoke a water-cooled hookah or hubble-bubble, in which the tobacco is flavoured with palm syrup and coconut.

Travel in the south from Seenu Atoll to Gnaviyani Atoll — also known as Fua Mulaku and pronounced Foah Mulah — is often difficult. Angry squalls blow up suddenly and even well-anchored boats begin to toss and turn like angry horses at a tether. In such circumstances, a boat with an engine may avoid being swept upon the coral reef, but with only their lateen sail the traditional *dhoanis* are more vulnerable.

The Indian Ocean currents are the only ocean currents that change with the prevailing winds. Normally a one-and-half-knot current flows between Seenu and Gnaviyani. Local skippers have to take this into consideration when sailing in a north, north-east direction out of sight of land. When they leave an island Maldivians never look back. Their eyes search for a safe passage to the next landing, God willing. Only the flying fish skimming the waves break the monotony of the ever-changing but constant sea.

Out on its own in the middle of the Indian Ocean just below the

Equator, the island of Fua Mulaku must be one of the most isolated places in the world. Surrounded by a steep, coarse coral shingle beach, it is forty kilometres south of Gaafu Dhaalu Atoll (South Huvadhoo Atoll) and 430 kilometres from Malé. It has no sheltered mooring, and boats must anchor in the lee, away from the prevailing monsoon. During the north-west monsoon a small rowing boat (*bokkuraa*) comes out to collect visitors; pulling on their small triangular oars, only skilled fishermen are able to negotiate the pounding surf in the narrow channel that leads to the landing spot at Rasgefannu.

About six kilometres long and three kilometres wide, the island is the largest in Maldives. It has eight villages and a population of more than 7,000, although at any one time about 2,500 men may be working away from home.

Isolated though it might be, Fua Mulaku is blessed by nature and is one of the most fertile islands in Maldives. A wide variety of fruit and vegetables is grown: mangoes, watermelons, papayas, limes, bananas, oranges, and pineapples. Taro, known locally as *ala*, grows

Above: Carpenters or maavadin *build a* dhoani *from coconut planking for the carvel hull and local hardwoods for the frame. The hull used to be sewn together with coir but the planks are now secured with copper nails. A team of four or five carpenters can carve a standard ten-metre fishing* dhoani *with simple tools in about forty days. The basic design has not changed in centuries, and the master carpenter knows it so well that he needs no plans.*

Above: Jeweller fashions delicate necklaces and bracelets from imported gold and silver. The kerosene lamp in the glass jar is called a fulhi baththi*; a local invention, it is kept burning all night in most homes.*

so well that it is more important than rice as a staple food. The tropical vegetation is luxuriant and widespread. An areca-nut tree, looking like a date palm with betel sprouting from its trunk like a liana, grows in most compounds.

While each family has been given a compound by the government as their home, there is so much land available for cultivation that anyone who wishes can obtain a vegetable plot to cultivate. Although the government is the sole landowner, these plots are traditionally handed down through the families and tended by the womenfolk while the men go fishing.

As the island was once an atoll of three islands, it seems probable that at one time ships could sail right into the middle of the lagoon. As the entrance channels silted up to form one island, however, the rain washed away the saltwater of the enclosed lagoon and eventually left two freshwater lakes — Bandaara Kulhi and Dhadimage Kulhi. Several species of fish thrive in their warm waters, and at night bullfrogs splash and bellow in the shallows. The high water table allows taro to grow in the swamps around the lakes.

East and West found an early meeting place at Fua Mulaku. With its fresh fruit and unlimited water supply, Fua Mulaku was undoubtedly a favourite landing place for early seafarers passing through the Equatorial Channel.

Impressive ruins establish that Fua Mulaku has been inhabited for thousands of years. Near Hoadhandu Avah village, some 150 metres from the shore, a mound, or *hawitta*, about twenty metres high and seventy-five metres in circumference, was a bell-shaped Buddhist *stupa* on a square platform. Towering above the coconut trees, shining white in the Equatorial sun, it must have been a famous landmark. Islanders call this extraordinary monument *Redinge Funi*, that is, Redin's Hill.

Unfortunately, the original masonry has been removed from the *hawitta* on Fua Mulaku by locals for various purposes, but a few beautifully dressed stones remain scattered in the bush beneath the pandanus palms growing on the mound. The archaeologist, H. C. P. Bell, who visited the site in 1922, was unable to find the stone statue of a Buddha which he had been told lay there. Sixty years later, Thor Heyerdahl also visited the site and agreed with Bell's conclusion that it must have been a Buddhist *dagoba*, its round bell-shape covered in white plaster, not carved with ornaments — but local scholars do not accept these conclusions.

The stones of two small *hawittas* nearby have been scattered and plundered; some as stone boundaries around watermelon beds. Some time ago a small stone elephant was found near one of the small *hawittas*. Once there were also two statues — one of a woman, the other of a man holding a fish on a cord. The locals called the latter *Mahafothi Kaleyge* (The Owner of the Fish) and claimed that one day just as a fisherman was giving a fish to his wife a *jinni* passed by and threw coral sand at them, thereby turning them to stone. Both statues have long since disappeared.

In the Dhiguvann Mosque, a few hundred metres from 'Redin's

Hill', lies the body of Abdul Naib Kalegefan, the son of Yusuf Naib Kaleyfaanu, who first arrived with his brother but was killed, or martyred as the islanders put it. The mosque is built from ill-fitting carved and polished limestone slabs that were probably taken from an earlier temple on the site.

Near Dadimagu village, by another mosque called Kedeyre, a beautiful and original sunken enclosure with a stairway, marks a ceremonial bath about five metres square and 1.3 metres deep. Although it is made from blocks of different sizes, they are cut with such precision and fitted so carefully that it is impossible to push a knife between them. Excavating the floor of the bath, islanders uncovered a bench around the sides on which the people sat as cool, crystal-clear fresh water slowly filtered around them.

Despite the mounds of rubble and unwritten stories of the people, the mystery of Maldives remains unsolved. The origins of the people can never be fully known, any more than the number of polyps that go to make up a reef. Countless seafarers have touched its shores in the past, and now a new breed of traveller is arriving, but the footprints they leave in the sandy shore will be washed away by the ceaseless pull of the tide. What exists is like the tip of the reef; the rest has disappeared in the deep blue of time.

Generations of travellers have been bewitched by the outstanding beauty of Fua Mulaku. When Ibn Battuta stayed seventy days on the island of Muli in Meemu Atoll in 1344, waiting for the monsoon to change so that he could travel to the Malabar (Coromandel) Coast, the islanders were fearful of him and his crew. But on orders from the *wazir* in Malé they gave them cowries, coconuts, honey, betel, areca-nuts, and fish every day.

The French brothers Jean and Raoul Parmentier, who rounded the southern cape of Africa in the sixteenth century aboard *Pensée* and *Sacré*, landed on Fua Mulaku on 24 September 1529. They assumed that the devout man who welcomed them with lemons as offerings was the chief priest. They recorded:

In this island was a Temple or Mosque, a very ancient structure, composed of massive stone. The Captain desired to see the inside as well as the outside, whereupon the Chief Priest bade them to open it, and entered within. The work pleased him greatly; and chiefly a woodwork screen, with a balustrade so neatly turned that our ship's carpenter was surprised to see the fineness of the work.

The two Frenchmen were the only Europeans who visited Fua Mulaku before Bell landed on its shores and explored its ruins in 1922. He loved its 'bliss of solitude' and considered it the most beautiful island in the archipelago. He was followed in 1985 by Thor Heyerdahl who was no less affected by the peace and beauty of this lost isle in an azure sea.

Although electricity has come to the island and the fishing *dhoanis* have diesel engines, everyday life has changed remarkably little since Battuta's visit. Islanders are still superstitious, combining their faith in Islam with an older belief in spirits (*dhevi*). One *dhevi* called Aruffanu Fureytha, which first appeared to fishermen as a big,

Above: In the tropical climate of Gan Island in Seenu Atoll, frangipani flourishes and fills the air with its heady scent. Local women make perfume from its white flowers.

Above: Memorial to the Indian dead of World War Two at the old British airbase on Gan Island in Seenu Atoll.

glowing flame hovering over the sea at night, came ashore as a monster and killed people by sucking their blood. Legend has it that only when a master magician (*fanditha*) was brought in and cast a spell on the monster was it turned into a big boulder. It is still there on the reef and islanders claim that if it is struck with an iron bar blood will seep from it.

Until recently, the islanders of Fua Mulaku used to trade directly with Sri Lanka, sailing in large three-masted *odis* which had four square sails and one triangular sail. About fifteen metres long, five metres wide, and three metres high, these vessels travelled at two or three knots, but could reach ten to fifteen knots with a good wind. The crew consisted of the captain, bosun, and cook. The passengers, between twenty-five and thirty-five in all, slept on deck and were expected to lend a hand as crew.

The *odis* sailed to Sri Lanka on the south-west monsoon, carrying dried tuna fish, coconuts, and syrup made from the sap of coconuts. The passage took about six days. After a wait of some weeks for the monsoon to change, they returned on the north-east winds with rice, sugar, flour, cotton, and clothes.

The last voyage of a beautiful and ancient *odi* from Fua Mulaku took

Above: Mudhimu *(muezzin) teaches Meedhoo Island children the Qur'an in the local mosque. When they grow up, men and women attend different mosques for worship.*

Opposite: Flags of respect flutter around the well-kept tomb of a famous local Islamic leader among the broken tombstones of the long-forgotten dead.

place in 1978. Now that the diesel engine has made sail redundant for long voyages the only remaining trace left of the graceful and proud *odis* is the picture on Maldivian currency notes. For long-distance travel within the archipelago, there are smaller *baththeli*, about twenty metres long with two masts, a deckhouse, and an inboard engine, but more common are cargo vessels and safari *dhoani*.

Sailing in Maldives is dangerous for mariners who are unfamiliar with the reefs, and foreign mariners who enter the atolls without a pilot do so at their own peril. The most modern charts of Maldives, issued by the British Admiralty, carry the warning:

The depiction of the reefs and dangers is based almost entirely on a lead-line survey of l835. It is known that many uncharted dangers exist and that the positions and the shapes of many of the reefs are different from that shown. Mariners should navigate with extreme caution.

When approaching an island you sometimes see a rusty metal pole or tree branch, whitened by sun and sea, marking the channel through the shallows. Locals navigate with great care; a lookout in the bow strains hard to discern the slightest change in the colour of the sea-bed and gestures to the helmsman what direction to take to avoid submerged coral outcrops.

Even the most careful captain has heard the dreaded grinding sound of their wooden hull scraping the rugged coral. If he is lucky the vessel breaks free; if he is not, he must wait for the tide or help. The boats repaired on the beaches reveal the scars of their unavoidable fate.

Nonetheless, moving about on their tossing decks with great dexterity and balance, Maldivians are completely in their element at sea. And no wonder — many spend more time upright in a boat than on land.

Crossing the Equatorial Channel from Fua Mulaku to Gaafu Dhaalu Atoll is an eerie experience. During this forty-kilometre voyage you not only cross the Equator, moving from southern to northern hemisphere, but travel over an unknown sea-bed more than 1,300 fathoms below. Who knows what strange creatures or sunken ships lurk at those murky depths?

You also travel across a channel that has been used for centuries by mariners crisscrossing the Indian Ocean, from Africa to China, the Persian Gulf to Malaysia. They have travelled in Egyptian papyrus boats, Arab dhows, Chinese junks, windjammers, steamships, and modern tankers on one of the oldest and most used shipping ways in the world.

After the pink blush of dawn, the sun rises a glorious orange in the east and traces its straight trajectory across the heaven only to fall directly west into the silver sea. The sun dominates all, the flat azure of the sea and the blue dome of the sky. Directly overhead at its midday zenith, it dwarfs a lone man on his tiny piece of bobbing wood in the midst of the blue immensity.

The only company for the lonely mariner is an occasional school of dolphins which suddenly rushes at the boat to veer off into the

distance just as suddenly. When it seems they are about to be run down, the inevitable flying fish leap into the air for their ten-second glide. Frigatebirds, with their long, forked tails, or white-tailed tropicbirds, urged on by some strange dream unknown to man, pass overhead.

Currents run up to five knots, and the skipper who does not take this into account can easily be swept past the next atoll.

Normally Maldivians do not use a sextant but steer by compass, taking into account the currents and distance covered. They measure their speed by throwing a piece of coir into the sea. But while they base their course on dead reckoning between the atolls, they still look out for the clouds on the horizon that sometimes reflect the green of island foliage.

Seventy kilometres long by fifty-five kilometres wide, with a lagoon eighty-six metres deep, Huvadhoo Atoll covers 2,240 square kilometres and is the largest atoll in the world; so large, in fact, that for administrative purposes it has been split arbitrarily into Gaafu Dhaalu and Gaafu Alifu atolls.

Above: Morning lesson on a remote island in Gaafu Alifu Atoll. Every village has at least one of these privately run makthab *schools which takes pupils from the age of three and teaches them the three 'R's as well as the tenets of the Islamic faith.*

Above: Young girl learns to form her letters — in Dhivehi *and Arabic — on a wooden board scattered with fine sand.*

Like Seenu and Gnaviyani atolls, Huvadhoo also has its own dialect which most people from Malé cannot understand. Its isolation in the south and its own sense of cultural identity have made it proud of its independence and in the 1960s it was the centre of the cessionist movement that formed the separate but short-lived republic of the United Suvadive Islands.

Huvadhoo now benefits, however, from new government health centres and primary schools and the prosperity brought by tourism. But many men still have to go away to earn a living: about as many work in tourist resorts as engage in fishing.

When you travel north across the Equatorial Channel one of the first islands of Huvadhoo Atoll you come across is Vaadhoo. As with so many Maldivian islands, it is necessary to land from a small boat on a jetty across a shallow foreshore. Fishing is still important to the local economy of Vaadhoo. The stench of drying fish wafts across the water, and on the beach in the late afternoon fishermen boil black sea cucumbers in drums — a delicacy not eaten by Maldivians, but relished by Malaysians. Indeed, so great is the demand that in some areas the numbers of sea cucumbers are in sharp decline.

There too, the sudden appearance of a European is enough to create a look of shock and horror on the face of the young children and send them scurrying to the safety of their homes. The younger women, however, look calmly on, and do not lower their eyes in false modesty. Having learned English at the primary school, some of the bolder children reappear to say with cheeky smiles: 'Hello! How do you do?'

Islanders are proud of the fact that Sultan Muhammed Ibn Ali, who reigned over Maldives for eight years during the seventeenth century, came from Vaadhoo.

Vaadhoo has been found to be the site of early Buddhist worshippers, and the islands adjoining the Equatorial Channel in Gaafu Dhaalu are scattered with ruins and artefacts. On the island of Kon' dey, Thor Heyerdahl came across a limestone sculpture, as big as a cock and black with age, which turned out to be the head of the Hindu water god Makara, a demon often decorating the entrances to Hindu temples and seen as a projecting waterspout in sacred fountains.

The most impressive ruin, however, is on the uninhabited island of Gan next to Gadhdhoo. At first sight it seems strange that the inhabitants of Gadhdhoo should live on such a small island, while the neighbouring island of Gan is so much larger and empty. Gadhdhoo, only 400 metres long by 200 metres wide, has a population of about 2,000. It is so small that from the crossroads in the middle of the village, you can see the sea at the end of all four roads. The women weave beautifully intricate mats from a reed called *haa*, which grows on the island of Fioari.

In Sanskrit, *gamu* means village or settlement and there is an abandoned Islamic cemetery on the island. People from Gadhdhoo cross the narrow stretch of water to collect coconuts and firewood but do not stay on Gan overnight. They also bury their dead there if they have been sick or died at sea.

The island was deserted between 1779 and 1799. The people say that the island was invaded by huge cat-like spiritual beings who killed or chased away all the inhabitants. However, the process of resettlement of the island is currently underway.

From the middle of the jungle rise the ruins of a huge *stupa*, which dates back to the tenth or eleventh century, called *Vadiyaamagu Hawitta*. Each side of its square base measures twenty-three metres, making an enormous ground area of 529 square metres. During excavations in the early 1980s, Thor Heyerdahl found sun symbols like open eyes and squared blocks of stone with sun reliefs, sun flowers, and lotus flowers cut into them, scattered around the site. There was also the foot of a sitting Buddha statue, a stone bull, and two lions.

In its heyday this pyramid must have been an amazing sight, a huge pyramid of white limestone carved with marvellous designs standing in a clearing in the dense, green jungle and shining in the sun.

In 1599, after visiting Fua Mulaku, the Dutchman Frederick de Houtmann recorded coming across an extraordinary temple complex on an uninhabited island. Although it is impossible to pinpoint the island, the magnificence of the ruins recalls those on Gan Island:

The small island close to which we lay had many beautiful buildings, most in ruins, very artfully built after their fashion. There appeared to be all sorts of Temples and altars, which were there in that small space, fully from ten to twelve: among them one especially of an ancient structure, all of blue stone (azurite), and round it also mouldings, basements, capitals (pillars), friezes and their groovings [tandeerzel], *on the steps of the entrance breastways: and what surprised me most was that all this was put together without any lime or building material; yet everything so closely bound together by means of hewn grooves that the point of a knife could not be put between them, while at each corner a keystone held the entire work together.*

Round the temple was a rectangular wall, constructed with a broad walk around it, and outside this walk were also some wells built of stone, which were dry, and among these one which appeared to be a tank. There was also hard by a crumbled Pyramid, of which the basement or foundation was still to be seen. It was twelve feet square, and appeared to have been a beautiful work, for it seemed to have been made with mouldings, round and hollow and square, with groovings all in proportion.

All the temples stood East and West, the entrance being to the East. I thought it must have been a sacred place, as all these buildings stood close to each other.

Above: Tern alights on a rock of coral laid bare by the ebbing tide. There are at least fifteen types of resident sea bird in Maldives, most of which are terns, including the rare white or fairy tern. Islanders make pets of sea birds, as well as eating their flesh and eggs.

Thinadhoo, the capital of Gaafu Dhaalu, was once capital of the whole atoll and the short-lived United Suvadive Islands Republic. Inhabitants still recall the invasion of 4 February 1962. The town was flattened and the entire population banished to neighbouring islands, not returning until 22 August 1966.

Gaafu Dhaalu no longer trades directly with Sri Lanka, for all

Above: Aerial view of one of the larger resort islands with villas on the seashore and a clearing made for a football pitch.

transactions pass through Malé. But it enjoys the new prosperity that tourism has brought to the region and the capital boasts its own local 'five-star' guesthouse and several teashops.

An intriguing iron knob emerges from the sand in the garden of one resident. Workers abandoned an attempt to disinter it. After digging down two metres the iron pole would still not budge. It is said to have been buried there in the nineteenth century by Captain Moresby — who was responsible for drawing up the British Admiralty chart of Maldives which is still used today.

The capital of Gaafu Alifu (North Huvadhoo Atoll) is Viligili where there was once a big *hawitta*. Although a road called Hawitta Magu still exists, the ancient mound has long since been washed away by the sea. In 1982, however, Thor Heyerdahl came across a raft made from giant bamboo that had been washed up on its reef. Quite unlike any craft built in the archipelago, it must have drifted 3,000 kilometres from Burma.

Fishing is still the mainstay of the economy and most of the fishing *dhoanis* in these southern atolls are privately owned. The

day is long and hard for the fishermen must rise at five in the morning to catch reef fish with small nets to use as bait. The bait is kept alive in water in the bottom of the boats. Off to sea, the *dhoanis* travel for up to four hours, using their steady Japanese diesel engines if the wind does not fill their lateen sail, in search of shoals of tuna. In the old days, with their square sails made from palm matting, they were at the mercy of the winds.

Tracking shoals of tuna is difficult but birds circling in the sky often serve as a tell-tale clue. Now the real work begins. Squeezing the bait in their hands, the crew slip the stunned but wriggling fish overboard to attract the tuna. When the tuna begin feeding, the fishermen splash the water, making them more excited. They then cast their lines, loaded with feathered hooks, from long rods and whisk the unsuspecting tuna into the bottom of the boat. The hooks have no barbs so that the fish can be flipped off them easily. The action is fast. On good days, a single boat may catch a thousand tuna or more.

Later, muscles tired and throats dry after the day's strain and

Above: The closest man can get to the tropical frigatebird, exhilarated by the balmy sea breezes, and confident of a delightful landing in the warm waters of the Indian Ocean.

Following pages: Sheltered lagoons and gentle breezes make the resorts of Maldives ideal for novice and intermediate windsurfers and catamaran sailors.

Above: Parasailer in a multi-coloured parachute rides an azure Maldivian sky.

excitement under the merciless sun, comes the long haul home. The fishermen, who usually reach land in the late afternoon, carry the catch ashore to gut the fish before giving them to their womenfolk to dry or cook. Any excess will be dried for export or collected by one of the government freezer ships that move around the atolls, buying the fish directly from the returning fishermen for ready cash. It saves the long process of drying.

Boats are central to Maldivian life, essential for earning a living from fishing, collecting wood and coconuts from other islands, and for travel. Most families have at least one small *dhoani*, while richer families have several.

Made from coconut and local hardwood, the carvel boats are like sleek Arab dhows — long and slender, with elegant curving prows. In olden days their planks were bound together by coir, making them more flexible when passing over coral reefs. In the late thirteenth century, John of Montecorvino noted:

HiFly

Opposite: The variety of water sports offered by the Maldives' resorts is endless — and interesting, like this unusual 'water sausage' ride.

*Above: The white, or fairy, tern (*Gygis alba*) takes up a perch in a breadfruit tree. This graceful sea bird is found only in Seenu Atoll in the south where, according to local legend, its presence ensures the complete absence of crows on the atoll.*

Their ships in these parts are mighty frail and uncouth, with no iron in them and no caulking. They are sewn like clothes with twine. And so if the twine breaks anywhere, there is a break indeed. Once every year therefore there is a mending of this, more or less, if they propose to go to sea. And they have a frail and flimsy rudder, like the top of a table, a cubit in width, in the middles of the stern; and when they have to tack, it is done with a vast deal of trouble; and if it is blowing in any way hard, they cannot tack at all. They have but one sail and one mast, and the sails are either of matting or some miserable cloth. The ropes are of husk.

From about the sixteenth century, the system was replaced by one where ribs and hull were fastened together by wooden pegs because of the scarcity of iron nails.

Yet the Maldivians were always expert and courageous mariners. In their small boats, navigating by different stars by means of simple nautical instruments in lieu of points of the compass, they braved storms to sail as far as Sumatra, Penang, Calcutta, and Aden. A favourite Maldivian poem entitled *Dhioage Raivaru* goes:

Lo! our barque's upon the wave,
Dangers of the deep to brave,
Path 'mid ocean wilds to pave —
To Aden.

Guiding stars with kindly ray
Will direct us on our way
Through the darkness, day by day —
To Aden.

Seas of strife as wide as deep,
Restless waves that never sleep,
Currents of terrific sweep —
To Aden.

Slender barque of bosom's sail,
Breasting bold the sternest gale
Till near haven's light she hail —
To Aden.

The beautiful three-masted *odi* sailing ships made in Maldives were often seen in most Indian ports but, unfortunately, there is no longer any demand for them. *Dhoanis* are still made and the local carpenter (*maavadin*) is a highly respected member of the community. A team of four or five carpenters takes about forty days to build a standard *dhoani*, some ten metres long. Fishing *dhoanis* are about twenty-eight metres long. Until quite recently, the sails of the Maldivian *dhoanis* were square. Occasionally these are still seen in the southern atolls, although the triangular lateen sail is more common. Even this, however, is rapidly being superseded by diesel engine.

The clumsy looking replacement for the sleek *odi* is the cargo *dhoani*, which has a top-heavy superstructure rather like a box stuck on top of the sleek *dhoani* hull. Not surprisingly, they roll in the

Opposite: Water-skiing, Maldivian style.Warm, calm waters, tropical sun, and the most modern facilities ensure perfect recreation — and paradise for watersports enthusiasts.

Opposite: Moonbather finds relief from the day's Equatorial heat on the deliciously cool and moist sand, as the tide slowly ebbs and the moon drifts gracefully across the clear night sky.

slightest swell. However, they carry up to 200 passengers who sleep on deck among their belongings. Whatever their appearance, their arrival at an island is greeted with much enthusiasm and interest. Powered by diesel, some now travel as far as Sri Lanka and India, never having to worry about the monsoon winds, unlike their graceful ancestors.

Above: Islanders paddle their way home across the moonlit waters of the lagoon after visiting friends on a neighbouring island.

4. Diamonds in the Sun

The broadest stretch of water in Maldives is the One-and-Half-Degree Channel that runs between Gaafu Alifu Atoll and Laamu Atoll. It derives its name on maritime charts from its northern latitude, but it is known locally as Huvadhoo Kandu. Ninety-six kilometres wide, with a maximum depth of 1,130 fathoms, it is the widest and most dangerous of the channels that divide Maldives. During October and November currents run up to three and a half knots east, and from December to March, as the monsoon winds change direction, at almost four knots west.

On a calm crossing on a sunny day the sea may be a deep azure, the wake from the boat dancing like so many diamonds in the sun. In the afternoon, as the sun falls into the sky towards the west, the sea turns silver.

Frequently, however, the sky suddenly turns dark. A squall whips up white horses and the sea becomes a sinister, foaming blue-black. Many ships have missed their landfall, swept thousands of kilometres off course during the north-east monsoon.

Only a few frigatebirds, flying fish, and an occasional school of dolphin keep the little *dhoanis* company as they cross the channel. Without sophisticated navigation equipment, the crews constantly scan the horizon for the first hint of an island. Ocean-going tankers and cargo vessels frequently pass through the channel.

Finding the entrance into Laamu Atoll requires local knowledge, for all around the long swell of the Indian Ocean crashes onto the treacherous coral reefs. For a brief moment the water seems almost translucent as great turquoise waves curl gracefully in the sun only to crash in all directions onto the razor sharp coral.

Every mariner who crosses the One-and-Half-Degree Channel breathes a sigh of relief as they enter the inner lagoon to anchor near an island, rolling gently in the slight swell as their anchor cables strain at an angle of forty-five degrees to each other. The sights and sounds of land reach the tired crew: cries and laughter of children playing on the beach, flitting butterflies, and the surf breaking on the sand. The excitement and adventure of the sea give way to the comfort and security of the earth. One is as central as the other to Maldivian life.

Of course, in the flux of life nothing stands still. For centuries the Maldivians lived with their traditional ways and customs as if in aspic, but in the last few decades they have been hurled into the late twentieth century. Islanders, who are only just beginning to get used to the diesel engine and electricity, can now look up in the heavens and see the metal birds that land at the new airstrip on uninhabited Kadhdhoo Island — on their weekly migration to Gan in Seenu Atoll.

Laamu Atoll is about forty kilometres long and twenty-five kilometres wide. The capital, Hithadhoo, stands at the southern entrance to the atoll. Near the neighbouring island of Maamendhoo freezer ships often anchor for several weeks, collecting the daily catch from the atoll fishermen and acting as a floating bunker to supply fuel for their new diesel engines.

Bordering the One-and-Half-Degree Channel, Laamu Atoll has many ancient ruins like Huvadhoo Atoll. There are no less than three

Previous pages: Hull shadowed on the white coral sand beneath the deep crystal-clear waters, a bokkuraa *takes fishermen from their anchored* dhoanis *to a difficult landing on the rocky shore.*

Opposite: Coconut palms on the seashore slant almost horizontally out of the luxuriant tropical vegetation in eager search of life-giving sun on Buruni Island on Thaa Atoll. In the background is a bamboo raft from Burma which drifted unmanned on ocean currents across thousands of kilometres.

13743 7-E F

Opposite: Slender, classic lines of a Nilandhoo Island fishing dhoani *in Faafu Atoll, its beautifully curved bow reminiscent of ancient Phoenician and Egyptian craft. Maldivian fishermen are very superstitious and the flags are intended to bring good luck.*

Above: Boiling sea cucumbers in the late afternoon. Although Maldivians do not eat them, sea cucumbers are exported to Malaysia where they are considered a great delicacy.

mounds on Hithadhoo, although they are in a poor state, and others on Maabaidhoo, Mundoo, and Kadhdhoo. The most interesting, however, are those on Gan (Gamu) and Isdhoo.

To land at Gan (Gamu) you wade ashore from a small boat. The black crows on the beach contrast with the white coral sand. Large thatched sheds on the beach shelter boats under repair or construction. The wide avenues that crisscross the village, where about 2,000 people live, are shaded by lines of coconut palms and breadfruit trees. The paths are always immaculately clean, their white coral sand gleaming in the sun. Bananas, watermelons, papayas, and taro grow there. Women pound black millet (*bimbi*) with mortar and pestle for their babies, or rasp the pulp of coconuts for the evening curry.

Island life seems unchanged for centuries, but there are hints of modernity. Electricity has arrived and generators thump away. The new school built by the Japanese channels rainwater from its wide roofs into large storage tanks.

On the other side of the island lies evidence of a much earlier civilization. Close to the pounding surf, a crumbling mound of coral blackened by time, monsoon rains, and the tropical sun is called *haththeli*, meaning seven cooking pots, by the islanders.

This neglected monument of a bygone age stands about eleven metres high, and about fifty metres in diameter. In the tenth or eleventh century, glittering in the sun, this white temple towered over the surrounding palms. It is difficult to imagine the amount of labour required to cut and collect the coral slabs from the sea, haul them up to the mound, and then fit them together like pieces in a jigsaw puzzle.

Now the once proud temple is a sorry sight. Over the centuries its dressed stones have been pillaged to form the walls of buildings and the coral rubble used to make lime. Only one or two stones can still be discovered in the surrounding bush, their rectangular shape beautifully carved and precise. It will not be long before the sea washes away the last remains of these monuments to the sky in these remote islands near the Equator.

Although the islanders believe that these once enormous temples were built by the legendary Redin, the archaeologist H. C. P. Bell who visited Laamu Atoll earlier this century was convinced that the mounds were the ruins of Buddhist *dagobas* or *stupas*. Bell made an excavation of the mound on Gan (Gamu), which was then covered by tall trees. Now it is a denuded heap, but the large scar where he dug still runs down one side. He reported that although the temple had been stripped by the islanders it still had a seven-tier pinnacle on top which consisted of surface dressed madrepore slabs encasing a rubble core of the same material.

Since then the ravages of man have been crueller than nature, and all that remains is a pile of rubble. To smash up old pagan ruins for building material seemed much more sensible than cutting new coral blocks from the reef. Today, the temple is called by the same name that Bell recorded — *hatteli* — the pinnacle to which the term seven cooking pots presumably referred has long since disappeared.

Under the summit of the mound, Bell also discovered the broken face of an enormous Buddha and estimated its original height to be four and a half metres. On top of the pinnacle way above the coconut trees, shining white in the sun, it must have been an uncanny sight to lonely mariners from distant lands as they sailed through the One-and-Half-Degree Channel of the archipelago. There was also the headless image of a small seated Buddha below the face of the giant, but both remains have long since disappeared.

South-west of the great mound is a smaller *hawitta* with a circular bath close by. The island's first mosque was probably built on the monastery of the Buddhist monks, but it too has disappeared. It is possible that the Buddhists merely came and put a *stupa* dome on a stone-faced *hawitta*.

There is an even more impressive mound on the island of Isdhoo (the name means 'first sight'), in the most northerly tip of Laamu Atoll. Seen from the sea, rising far above the surrounding coconut palms, it is awe-inspiring. Strategically placed, the mound served as a landmark for ancient mariners travelling through the channels between the atolls. Also called *hatteli*, it stands near two smaller

Above: On Ribudhoo Island in Dhaalu Atoll, a jeweller's wife proudly displays a traditional gold necklace, rarely made nowadays. Although the veil, or purdah, *has never been part of the Islamic tradition in Maldives, an increasing number of devout women now cover their heads.*

Above: In his coral-walled workshop, a Ribudhoo Island jeweller fashions custom-made rings, earrings, bracelets, and necklaces from imported gold and silver. Maldivian jewellers are renowned for their delicate and refined craftsmanship.

hawittas nearby. The base of a one-metre-high statue of Buddha lies discarded in the bushes.

The island's 300-year-old mosque was probably built on the foundations of an older temple.

Travelling across the inner waters of Laamu Atoll on a quiet day under the bright tropical sun is a magical experience. Small green islands dot the horizon all around and the water is as calm as a mill pond and as clear as glass. Shoals of jellyfish float by and small, bright blue neon fish dart in all directions. The ever-present flying fish, which leap out of the water just as they are about to be run down, glide effortlessly for about fifty metres in twelve seconds — small or large, they seem to cover the same distance in the same time. The only problem on such a day is that it is difficult to see the shallow reefs; the flat sea reflects the light of the sun and the crew cannot detect the subtle changes in the colour of the sea-bed that warn of danger.

North of Laamu lies Thaa Atoll (Kolhumadulu Atoll), virtually a circular reef enclosing 700 square kilometres of sea. There are only a few points of entry and the many submerged reefs, especially in the south and west, make navigation dangerous even for shallow-draught *dhoanis*. On the eastern side, many tiny desert islands can be reached by wading from one to the other through the turquoise water.

Thaa contains one of the largest islands in the archipelago — uninhabited Fahala, which is covered with dense vegetation. The capital island, Veymandhoo, has grown prosperous on the rich harvest of fish that the seas yield in this region. The most populous island, however, is Thimarafushi, even though it was swept by mysterious fires in 1902 and 1905 that razed all buildings and vegetation.

Dhiyamigili Island is of historical interest as the birthplace of Muhammed Imaaduddeen II, the eighteenth-century sultan who founded a dynasty that lasted for about sixty years. The ruins of his residence lie outside the village. Another monument on Guraadhoo Island marks the grave of Sultan Usman who was banished to the island in the fourteenth century after ruling for only two months.

On the most northerly island, Buruni, the pull of Malé is strong — a quarter of the men work away as carpenters and builders or in the tourist resorts. Most of those who remain practise fishing. The women weave mats from reeds and make rope from coir.

The island has long been inhabited. The tombs in the cemetery surrounding the Burunee Ziyaaraiy Mosque are more than 190 years old. An old sundial outside the mosque told the *mudhimu* when it was time to call the faithful to prayer, but now a modern Chinese clock ticks away in the *mihraab*. Electricity has arrived on the island and the *mudhimu*'s voice vies with the sound of radio sets and the lure of videos. Island life is changing irrevocably.

Buruni, however, will remain famous in Maldives for the legend of a girl called Dhon Hiyala whose father, a low-caste toddy tapper (*raaveri*), was raised to a higher rank by the sultan because of his proficient recital of the Qur'an. Dhon Hiyala fell in love with a

jeweller, called Ali Fulu, who gave her beautiful ornaments. But their love was star-crossed. When the sultan's agents seized her because of her beauty and took her to court in Malé, her incensed lover followed and rescued her. The lovers fled in a boat but were pursued by the sultan's soldiers and when the couple jumped into the sea to escape, they were devoured by a demon.

Today on Buruni such legends seem anachronistic when you come across smart young men in Western clothes who speak fluent English. Some may tell you that they are 'on holiday' but in fact many of these youngsters have been banished from resort islands for transgressing Islamic law and drinking alcohol. Banishment can serve well the wrongdoers and the communities in which they live. They are not isolated with other hardened criminals and have an opportunity to be useful to their new neighbours. If they are educated, the islanders can also learn from them.

The island chief (*katheeb*) works with an island committee that usually consists of five appointed members and five elected by the islanders. They make no key decisions but together decide how to

Above: Islander in fashionable beachware acquired from close association with the tourist trade, takes a professional look at a traditionally built dhoani *under cover from the beating sun, within easy reach of the water's edge.*

Above: Model dhoani *with its elegantly curved prow and tiller, made from mother of pearl. An increasing number of islanders are abandoning fishing to make souvenirs for the visiting tourists.*

implement government policy and resolve practical issues such as distributing electricity or organizing a census.

In the last decade, life has gradually improved. Twenty years ago the outlying atolls had no doctors or modern health services. Now, with health centres in all the atolls, health care programmes reach the most remote villages. Nevertheless, some islanders still suffer from filaria and leprosy, and there are occasional outbreaks of dengue fever, but malaria which in the past laid so many travellers low has been eradicated, according to Maldivian officials.

Islanders also rely on traditional medicine men and women who have developed knowledge from contact with Indians, Arabians, Persians, Malaysians, Sri Lankans, and Chinese, synthesizing their own herbal remedies. Legends abound about the feats of special healers, such as Buraki Ranin, the queen of Sultan Muhameed in the sixteenth century. She was said to be able to cure sword wounds overnight with her own dressings. Such knowledge has become systematized and the treatise written by Shaikh Hussain of Meedhoo from Seenu Atoll, who died in 1916, forms the foundation of today's traditional medicine.

Known as *hakeems*, practitioners are well-respected by the village communities. The basic tenet of their philosophy is that good health is the result of a proper balance between the hot, cold, and dry 'humours' in the body, so 'cold food' is recommended for someone with fever, and dry fish for flu. Some *hakeems* are schooled in *Unani* medicine, which treats the whole person, and combines ancient remedies with new drugs. In recent years there has been an attempt to integrate traditional and modern medicine; advice and training, for instance, is offered to local midwives who learned their skill from older practitioners.

Most children are still educated in local, privately owned schools (*makthab*) run by an Islamic teacher. From the age of three, children study in a large room or under a tree learning their alphabet with a wooden board covered in fine sand on which they trace their letters with a stick, or learning sections from the Qur'an by rote. They also learn to read and write *Dhivehi* and some Arabic as well as simple arithmetic. For centuries this was the only schooling available.

New government primary schools, however, have been built in the atolls with foreign assistance. These schools are so new that many headmasters have only just graduated themselves. Standards are demanding. By the age of seven pupils are expected to speak and write three languages with three different alphabets — *Dhivehi*, Arabic, and English. At present the emphasis on Arabic and English is about equal.

Hopping from one familiar island to another, it is very easy to forget that there are vast expanses of ocean on either side of the Maldivian archipelago and that the nearest land is thousands of kilometres away. There are, however, occasional reminders of the enormous distances seafarers undertook to reach the coral beaches of these tropical islands.

Early in 1990, for instance, a large bamboo raft with a covered living space quite unlike any vessel used in the Maldives, was

washed ashore on Buruni Island. No one was on board but there were the remains of a charcoal fire. Empty sugar sacks tied onto the deck revealed that it had come from Bangkok. In 1981, Thor Heyerdahl found a similar raft on Viligili, in Gaafu Alifu Atoll, that had drifted 4,000 kilometres from the coast of Burma. Whales have also been washed ashore.

Across the Kudahuvadhoo Channel, to the north-west of Thaa Atoll, lie two smaller atolls, Dhaalu (South Nilandhoo) and Faafu (North Nilandhoo). Tidal races stream east and west through the channel with the flood and ebb. Deflected by the atolls on either side, these currents are unpredictable and extremely powerful. In 1879, the master of the 1,340-tonne vessel *Liffey* found this out when he was shipwrecked on the reef of Kudahuvadhoo Island, at the most southerly tip of Dhaalu Atoll.

Inhabited for millenniums, Kuda Huvadhoo is now the capital of the atoll. It has an intriguing mound, twenty-two metres in diameter, in the jungle, and in the nearby mosque — the oldest on the island — villagers came across the stone head of a Buddha, almost two metres in diameter.

In the rear wall of the mosque, Thor Heyerdahl noted the finest 'fingerprint' masonry he had ever seen.

Above: Freshwater wells and convenient stepping stones outside an ancient mosque where the devout wash themselves before entering the mosque to offer prayers. The dressed stones are probably taken from a pre-Islamic temple but the hot tin roof is an unfortunate modern addition.

Above: Buruni Island's drifting coral sands half bury a beautifully carved tombstone in the cemetery of a 190-year-old mosque. Tragically, the stone-carving skills which created such a work of art have already been lost.

Set in this smooth stone wall was a block, roughly one metre square, with its facade as carefully planed as if cut and polished by a machine; but all around the edge, cut into twelve sides with complex corners, everything fitted so precisely into the complex shapes of the surrounding stones that the fissures would barely show up in a photograph. It was incredible to find such a masterpiece of stone-shaping art here.

In front of the mosque is an outdoor gateway, similar to the one on Nilandhoo. On the outer wall is a perfect six-pointed star, known locally as *Suleiman mudhi*, the seal on King Solomon's ring.

Two beautifully fashioned and decorated tombstones inside the mosque cemetery are the work of the master mason who is reputed to have done the superb stone in the mosque wall. The top of each tombstone has five points. Muslim ones always carry only one point on the top of the stone for a man while a woman's tombstone remains rounded. Inscriptions are also carved on them in flowing Arabic.

Certainly, Maldivian stone carvers have an ancient tradition

Opposite left: Smiling Maldivian toddler enjoys swinging on the undhoali *of his immaculately clean family compound.*

Opposite: Girl's work: collecting water from a mosque well. While rainwater flows into the central depression on islands, it often tastes very salty. Locals say that it is good for the skin and do not like to wash in pure rainwater.

Above: Fisherman's daughter, head covered out of respect, reads verses from the Holy Qur'an next to her father's sails.

Opposite left: Pounding locally grown bimbi *(millet) on Gan (Gamu) Island in Laamu Atoll. Although millet is highly nutritious, most Maldivians prefer imported rice which takes much less effort to prepare.*

Opposite: Thaa Atoll islander making thatch with coir from coconut fronds. It is mainly used for partitions and walls, although nowadays people who can afford it prefer to build with coral.

which has been lost only in this century. In the Arab world Maldivians were justly famous for producing the finest Muslim tombstones found anywhere. The tragedy is that along with the lost skills, many ancient tombstones throughout the archipelago have been broken, often repaired with grotesque smears of cement that have obliterated the delicate and flowing filigree work.

Many islanders, unaware of their unique architectural heritage, happily plundered the site for stone to build their own houses, but uninhabited Maadheli Island, also known as Salazar and Temple Island, has ruins whose riches have yet to be explored.

The government now forbids anyone to remove stones from these ancient ruins and mounds, and no one is allowed to explore or excavate them without special permission. The universal value of these unique splendours is at last being appreciated.

Ribudhoo Island and its satellites in the north of Dhaalu Atoll are shown on the British Admiralty chart as 'Jewellers' Islands', so-called because apparently many years ago a sultan in Malé banished his chief jeweller to the atoll for producing gold plating and stealing the gold given to him. There the banished goldsmith taught his rare skills to the islanders who have passed them down from father to son ever since. Now Ribudhoo and the neighbouring islands are famous for the delicate craftsmanship they display in producing gold and silver necklaces, bracelets, and chains. These days, however, instead of working in gold or silver many produce jewellery for the tourist trade from black coral collected from the reef, where it grows only at a depth of thirty metres, by scuba divers who come from Malé.

The whole family is involved in production. Small lathes grind and polish the coral to the appropriate shape for beads and other styles. The entire island is dotted with small workshops where two or three members of the same family, working cross-legged in the shade of a coconut tree, are philosophical about the sudden and lucrative demand for black coral jewellery. As one observed:

Maldivian people do not think of the future; they think only of today. They are very cool. If the wind blows on to the south of the island, they go there. If it blows on the other side, they go there. Today we make black coral jewellery because it is easier to make and there is more profit; there is no casting and all you need is a few files. Tomorrow, if there is no market, we will go back to our old ways.

With the development of tourism, however, most men have abandoned fishing although the few who do venture out of the atoll in a five-man *dhoani* often return with a thousand fish or more. The *dhoanis* are built on the beach under cover of coconut fronds to protect the carpenters from rain and sun. Coconut planks are used for the carved hull, while the mast is made from the hardwood of the banyan tree. Although two-horsepower Japanese-built engines have replaced sailpower, a lateen sail made from one-foot strips of cotton is still carried in case of breakdown or particularly good winds.

Lying north of Dhaalu Atoll only five islands of the slightly smaller Faafu Atoll are inhabited, with Magoodhoo in the south as the

capital. Its neighbouring island, Dharaboodhoo, was a famous turtle-breeding ground where the females laid their eggs in the sand during the south-west monsoon from May to November.

Unfortunately, so many eggs end up on the family table, and the shells in the tourist shops, that fewer and fewer of these great antediluvian creatures return each year. This endearing, harmless, and little-understood species — whose breeding cycle still remains a mystery — now faces extinction. Scuba divers claim that turtles have a high degree of intelligence and tell of the creatures communicating directly with them, not only by giving divers lifts on their backs but also joining them in playful mood.

One of the important archaeological sites in Maldives is on Nilandhoo, an island in the south of Faafu Atoll at the centre of the archipelago, which is reached on a broad swell through a shallow coral reef. Thor Heyerdahl, accompanied by Mohamed Ibrahim Loutfi, uncovered a buried temple on the island where many phallic sculptures were discovered.

Heyerdahl concluded that this vast temple complex — the

Above: Welcoming mosque on Buruni Island in Thaa Atoll. Its cool, clean, and silent interior is a haven from the baking Equatorial sun.

Following pages: One of the joys of a voyage through Maldives: the discovery of yet another unspoilt tropical island — Buruni in Thaa Atoll — with a perfect lagoon and towering coconut palms.

Above: Decaying interior of the 300-year-old Friday Mosque on Isdhoo Island in Laamu Atoll. The lacquered supports, finely carved rafters, and the flowing calligraphy reflect the high degree of craftsmanship that once flourished on these remote islands in the middle of the Indian Ocean.

remaining foundations in the middle of the village measure about 115 by 170 metres — was built by Hindus, for phallus worship is unknown in Buddhism and Islam. Only Hindu worshippers carved *lingam* sculptures — the phallic image of the god Shiva. Heyerdahl and his team also excavated many little limestone carvings, like towers of umbrellas.

What little remains suggests the original temple was extremely impressive. Beautifully cut facing stones placed over a compact core of coral sand formed a kind of pyramid, facing the sun with a walled ramp on one side. The stepped pyramid may have been topped by a small domed temple, for some limestone fragments with carvings like the early Greek triglyph and metope designs were found on the site. Finely carved stones from some earlier structure had been thrown in with the fill.

Carbon dating implies that the pyramid, or ziggurat, was rebuilt about AD 550. In all it seems that there were seven similar temples on the site and Thor Heyerdahl also unearthed the ruins of a gate which might have been one of seven that surrounded the complex.

Above: Fisherman's son helps with nets outside his coral built house in Faafu Atoll.

Earlier this century, three mysterious stone boxes little more than thirty centimetres square are said to have been found in the area. One contained a golden cock and a metal plate with writing that no one could decipher. However, there is no evidence these relics exist anywhere today.

Standing on the site of the temple on Nilandhoo is the second-oldest mosque in Maldives, which was ordered by Sultan Muhammad Ibn Abdullah in 548 AH after he had completed the first mosque in Malé. Known as the Aasaari Miskiy (Old Friday Mosque), this magnificent structure of well-cut stone is decorated inside with marvellous wooden carvings in arabesque. The dressed stones were taken from the earlier temple. For such a small community, the mosque is extraordinarily large.

A large U-shaped stone outside the mosque is carved with a floral design. The last of two such stones, its original purpose has long been forgotten, but until recently it was used to hold the long thin pole with a can tied to the end that worshippers lower into the deep well for water to wash before offering prayers.

When Maldives converted to Islam, the temples and their statues

Above: Becalmed without an engine, lateen sail flapping gently, fishermen take to the timeless alternative to get out of the lee of the island.

made an obvious target for the sultan who travelled from Malé and symbolically razed them to the ground. And the stones were ideal building materials for the first mosque in the archipelago outside the capital.

Stretching south-west of Faafu Atoll, only nine of Meemu Atoll's (Mulaku Atoll) thirty-five islands are inhabited. The north-western side is entirely deserted. The capital, Muli, is the main fishing centre, while Kolhufushi and Mulaku islands have enough arable land to grow yams. One of the most interesting islands, Dhiggaru, boasts a teashop (*sai hotaa*), traditionally a male domain, which is run entirely by women. Called Hotel Rehendi, after one of the early Maldivian sultanas, it is operated by the women's association of the island and all the profits go to develop their projects.

Shaped like a boot, Vaavu (Felidu Atoll), the next atoll to the north, is separated from Meemu by the Vattaru Channel. Only five of its nineteen islands are inhabited and Felidhoo, the capital, still relies on fishing for its livelihood. Further north, however,

Opposite: Inviting waters are often treacherous, hence the need for markers to show the channel through the coral reef to the shelter of the inner lagoon of Thaa Atoll.

Left and above: Relaxing, European style, at the warm water's edge.

resort country begins. The islands of Alimatha and Diggiri cater to scuba divers and sun-lovers from northern climes.

Indeed, Vattaru reef, which nearly bursts through the sea to form another atoll, is one of the finest underwater diving spots in Maldives. While the monsoon-driven waves steadily erode Rakeedhoo, the atoll's most southerly island, several new islands are appearing among the sand banks on Vattaru reef. Mariners should steer well clear.

5. Flying Fish and Playful Dolphins

From the southernmost island of Maldives to the most northerly there is a distance of almost 1,000 kilometres. Although they are covered in luxuriant green vegetation, there are generally fewer coconut groves in the northern atolls. Their outer rims are often broken by deep, narrow channels, making it easier for the fishing *dhoanis* to pass in and out. The free-flowing ocean currents also result in healthy coral reefs and thriving marine life. But the weather in these parts is more unpredictable than in the south. In the past, devastating storms have washed away whole islands. One storm, on 7 May 1812, is still remembered. More recently, the cyclone that broke on 9 January 1955 caused immense damage.

Closer to southern India than to Sri Lanka, the influence of the subcontinent is also that much stronger in the north. In the past there were close contacts with the Lakshadweep (formerly Laccadive) Islands to the north, now part of India, which were largely dependent on the Raja of Cannanore. But while the closer proximity of the islands means that many are more interdependent than those in the south, island life is virtually the same.

As in the south, sailing between the islands is pure delight, with flying fish taking off to avoid the bows of the boats. In the evening, children play and shout on the beach, as fishermen wade ashore with the day's catch. Under the shade of large *cadjan* shelters, carpenters build and repair boats. In the family compounds smoke rises from the kitchens as the women prepare the evening meal.

Despite the small compass of each island, there are always surprises. As you set out to explore your new landfall, you might be invited to a *kaiveni sai* for a newly married couple. Music blaring from a house with a crowded courtyard may mean that some boys have been recently circumcised and are enjoying special treatment and privileged status while they recover. It is also possible to come across a *mawloodh*, a Muslim recital in Arabic that often goes on for days on end, with relays of readers. Although the texts are incomprehensible to the average islander these recitals are held in great awe.

Separated from Malé Atoll by the Kashidhoo Channel, Lhaviyani Atoll (Faadhippolhu Atoll) lies about eight hours north of Malé by motorised *dhoani*. Nearly all the small islands that make up the atoll are deserted; out of sixty only four have been settled. But with a total population of about 7,000 the villages are large. Naifaru, the capital with more than 2,000 inhabitants and a busy harbour, lies on the western rim. Nearby Hinnavaru, which is about the same size, also enjoys the new prosperity brought by the expanding tourist and fishing industries. Kuredhdhoo, the most remote of all the resort islands, 130 kilometres from Malé, is particularly popular with scuba divers.

Many fishermen there operate engine-driven *dhoanis* and freezer ships collect their tuna for the canning factory at Felivaru. Opened in 1977 as a joint venture with the Japanese, the factory, which is now owned by the Maldivians, exports between 15,000 and 18,000 tonnes of 'Made in Maldives' tuna a year. The quality is so high that it is sold in Europe's and Japan's finest supermarkets. Like the garment factory on Gan in the south, however, lack of local labour means that expatriate workers from Sri Lanka man the production lines.

Previous pages: Time to wash and relax aching muscles after a gruelling day's fishing under the relentless sun. Fishermen are often away from their islands from sunrise to sunset.

*Opposite: Betel plant (*bileh*) growing up the trunk of a coconut tree. Eaten with sliced areca-nut and cloves between and after meals, its leaves are considered a great stimulant. The great Arab traveller Ibn Battuta said of the ingredients: 'They sweeten the breath and aid digestion, prevent the disagreeable effects of drinking water on an empty stomach, and stimulate the faculties'.*

Above: Carrom, *a cross between shove-halfpenny and billiards, in which discs are flicked by the forefinger on a polished board in an attempt to down others in the corner pockets.*

While North American consumers enjoy yellow-fin tuna, Europeans prefer the smaller skipjack tuna. Connoisseurs claim that Maldivian skipjack is the best in the world. As the monsoon winds turn from the north-east to the south-west, the tuna follow the currents across the Indian Ocean. Despite the fleets from Seychelles that sweep the seas with voracious purse seine nets, these migratory fish are still abundant.

Two atolls called Baa and Raa (South and North Maalhosmadulu atolls), which are separated only by a narrow channel, stretch out to the west of Lhaviyani Atoll. Fulhadhoo, Fehendhoo, and Goidhoo — a string of islands just below Baa — have had more than their fair share of exiles and castaways, some of them highly unusual. In February 1963, in an inexplicable mystery of nature, almost four million flying fish soared out of the sea to their death on Goidhoo. Possibly the Redin were there too, for the heap of gravel and sand — one metre high and thirteen metres in circumference — in the centre of the island has yet to be fully explored.

Fulhadhoo is where the French explorer François Pyrard was shipwrecked in 1602 when his ship *Corbin* went aground on the reef, resulting in the fascinating account of his stay which lasted more than

Above: Six-year-old boys recover after circumcision, the principal ceremony in their lives. During their convalescence, their families put on a party for three days, with decorations, music, plenty of food, and visits from friends and neighbours.

Overleaf: Salted fish — lonu mas *— drying in the sun on Landhoo Island in Noonu Atoll is usually exported to neighbouring countries.*

five years. He was held captive by the sultan. Indeed, his movements were so closely watched that he could find no way to escape:

Few Europeans ever so much as touch there and none go to reside unless they are unfortunately cast away as I was and even in that case it is most likely they never get away.

With some companions he finally managed to escape when a fleet from Bengal suddenly arrived; at the sight of the vessels, the island king and his retinue fled, but the French castaways managed to get aboard the vessels. Despite his joy at getting away, Pyrard at least appreciated the boldness and skill of the Maldivians as sailors:

The natives have a wonderful dexterity in avoiding dangerous places. I have seen them sail so nicely as to rub upon rocks on both sides without any damage. Both the rich and the poor are inured to the sea from their infancy and fear not to encounter the most turbulent and foaming seas in little boats and barks, the number of which is unaccountable, for the poorest man that is has one and the rich have several.

Notwithstanding this expertise, the difficulties of navigating between the bars and reefs of the outer rim of the atolls and the dangerous pull of the currents that swing around to follow the monsoon winds have caused many mariners to be shipwrecked and lose their goods and sometimes their lives. Fortunately, from an early age Maldivians are very good swimmers.

Because of their extreme isolation, these remote islands are ideal for banished criminals. Fulhadhoo, Fehendhoo, and Goidhoo were open prisons from 1962 until very recently.

After stabbing his girlfriend to death in a fit of passion at a small guesthouse in Malé in 1976, one German visitor ended up on Fulhadhoo. Despite attempts by the German government to extradite him, he has since become a Muslim, married a local girl, and started a family. He had the choice to return to Germany to face trial, but preferred the immensity of sea and sky around his tropical island prison to the four walls of a cell in cold Europe.

He is treated no differently than any other banished Maldivian; if he earns his keep and behaves himself, then the local community will look after him. As a reformed character, he is even allowed to island hop.

Other countries with harsher penal codes might well learn from Maldives. Few banished wrongdoers commit a second crime. By remaining in society and doing something worthwhile, instead of being isolated with other criminals in prison, they learn not only social awareness but regain their self-respect. Banishment becomes a 'school of life', not a 'university of crime'.

In Baa Atoll there is the usual scarcity of adult males. Most are away working in Malé or the resorts, or sailing with a shipping line. The exception is the island of Thulhaadhoo where virtually everybody is involved in the production of the lacquerware (*lielaa jehun*) for which Maldives is justly famous. The village has expanded so fast it now occupies the whole island. In a desperate attempt to enlarge the island everything that can be thrown away is being dumped at the landing point for reclamation of land from the sea. The smell is unpleasant but

Above: Filleting tuna in Felivaru Canning Factory in Lhaviyani Atoll. Maldivian skipjack tuna is considered by connoisseurs to be the best tasting in the world. Most ends up in the supermarkets of Europe and Japan. The tuna is brought to the factory by freezer ships which collect the fish from fishermen in the atolls.

the villagers seem willing to pay this price for more elbow room.

In the narrow alleyways of the village, craftsmen sit cross-legged on the ground working away at different stages of their craft: shaping the boxes with axes; rubbing yellow, black, and red sticks of resin imported from India onto the boxes as they spin round on hand lathes; finally hand carving the intricate floral patterns. Traditionally made from local wood — Alexandrian laurel (*funa*) — the most impressive boxes are the large and circular dishes with elaborate designs on their lids which are used for family feast days.

The capital, Eydhafushi on the other side of the Baa Atoll, used to be famous for weaving heavy, white cotton sarongs with brown and black strands (*feyli*), but the craft is dying out among the old people. The black synthetic sarongs on sale in the local shops are much cheaper — and easier to wash.

The recent advent of electricity on the island keeps young cyclists on the streets at night and enables school children to do homework. For the first time in their history, it is not automatic for the rising generation to do exactly the same work as their fathers. As an earlier generation of

Top: One of many tropical plants in the symphony of blue, green, and white that makes up Maldives.

Above: Brightly coloured hibiscus, one of the many flowers decorating the gardens of islanders. There are only about 600 species of flora so far identified in Maldives, with fewer than 260 fully naturalized species. Many plants may have drifted on currents from the Pacific Ocean to Maldives.

stone carvers discovered, blacksmiths and jewellers may soon find themselves without apprentices.

As the capital of the atoll, Eydhafushi is the venue for one of the big events of the year — the finals of the inter-atoll soccer competition when supporters from the surrounding islands sail across to cheer on their teams. The game begins in the late afternoon as the sun's rays begin to slant through the lengthening shadows of the palm trees.

Played under FIFA rules, the most keenly fought games often finish with a nail-biting session of penalties to decide the outcome at the end of extra time. The fierce rivalry on the pitch is followed by a delicious street dinner of curries and desserts put on for the players by the locals. Although cricket is played on Malé, soccer is by far the most popular sport in Maldives. Indeed, earlier this century a Malé sultan ordered that every island should have a football field.

Although Maldivians work exceptionally hard to survive in their difficult maritime environment, they also enjoy their leisure. The clichéd vision of Maldives as a nation of 'lotus eaters' waiting for coconuts to fall from the sky or fish to flop on the beach is a complete myth, despite the Tourist Ministry boast that Maldives is 'where we teach you the art of doing nothing'.

Nonetheless, virtually everyone enjoys sport and dancing. Island elders spend a great deal of time playing cards in the shade of the village breadfruit tree or under a *cadjan* roof by the seashore. Chess is another favourite game, played extremely fast and with great gusto. The stylized pieces are banged down hard on the wooden board. But perhaps the most favourite pastime is simply to sit under a tree in a hammock made from coir net, or on a flat wooden swing in the house.

Many children learn arithmetic by playing a board game called *ovvalhu* in which cowrie shells are placed in sixteen different bowls carved into a wooden block. The game, which is similar to *bau*, probably originated in Africa. Children also play a board game — probably Arabic in origin — known as *carrom* in which they strike flat discs with their forefingers and try to knock discs into the four corner pockets, as in billiards.

Suppressed Maldivian emotions find expression in popular music and dance. The most common form of music and dance, *bodu beru*, is performed with drums made from the hollowed-out trunks of the coconut palm, traditionally covered in manta ray skin or the lining of shark stomachs. Half a dozen drummers, with two lead drummers, sit on the ground. Others join in by clapping their hands in rhythm.

One drummer leads the singing, while the rest join the chorus. Suddenly, individual dancers take the floor, gyrating slowly but working themselves towards the crescendo as the rhythm and singing increase in tempo, until finally they throw themselves around in a wild frenzy.

Stooped old men, desiccated by years of fishing under the merciless sun, catch a stray rhythm and throw themselves into the arena. With wild applause from the audience, they float and gyrate and grimace in their dance, passing on secret affinities from their ancestors. Although light bulbs and not the stars and moon now light the scene, and the skin on the coconut palm drum is made from plastic,not shark belly skin, the spirit is as authentic as ever.

In the *thaara*, the wildest island dance, the dancer stabs himself in the

Above: Specialist's touch; spinning coir rope from the fibres of coconut husks. Several strands are woven together to make very strong and buoyant rope long sought after by seafarers of the Indian Ocean.

back of the neck with an iron spike when he reaches the climax. Although the government has banned the *thaara*, such practices are still common among Hindus in Sri Lanka, and some say the dance still continues in the more remote northern atolls of Maldives.

Earlier this century, spear dancing was often performed before the sultan on special occasions but the archaeologist H. C. P. Bell, for one, was unimpressed by the 'series of stereotyped braggart posturings in front of one another, representative of single combat, which soon pall to the uninitiated Western spectator'. However, he enjoyed the stick dancing which was 'at least quaint, if not unpleasing'. (Bell was probably referring to the *dhandi jehun* in which groups of men tap out the rhythm with tiny sticks.)

The *thaara*, a rarely seen dance these days, was probably introduced from the Middle East some time in the seventeenth century. While others dance between them, singing in Arabic, a line of men sit on the ground and beat hand drums.

Another dying music form is the *raivaru*, a kind of poetic song that follows a strict metre, sometimes accompanied by a slow dance; very

Above: Making coir rope at Kulhudhuffushi, capital of Haa Dhaalu Atoll. After soaking coconut husks for three months or so in brackish water, they are beaten with a heavy piece of wood to release the fibres which are then dried in the sun before being spun into rope by hand.

much a distinctive creation of Maldivian culture. Some old fishermen at the helm still sing them on moonlit nights. In the evenings, after the day's work is done, you might hear the poignant lament of a *raivaru* singer on an anchored *dhoani*. Women also sing them as lullabies or love songs.

Only a two-kilometre-wide channel separates Baa from Raa Atoll, which has about ninety islands that stretch sixty kilometres northwards. The atoll has played an important part in the history of Maldives. According to legend the island of Rasgetheemu in the north is the original 'King's Island', where Koimala Kalo first lived when he arrived with the king's daughter from Sri Lanka nearly two millenniums ago. Subsequently, in about AD 1100, Koimala and his wife migrated to Malé, and settled there with the consent of the aborigines of Giraavaru Island, then the most important community in Malé Atoll.

The first time Ibn Battuta landed on the islands he stayed for ten days on Kinolhas in the south-east of Raa Atoll. He later recalled:

When I arrived at these islands I disembarked on one of them called Kannal's, a fine island containing many mosques, and I put up at the house of one of the pious persons there. On this island, I met a man called Muhammad, belonging to Dhafár, who told me that if I entered the island of Mahal the Wazir *would detain me there, because they had no* qadi.

This is precisely what happened. The honour and hospitality he received in Kinolhas and the neighbouring islands persuaded him to visit Malé. After visiting Malé, Battuta intended to sail to Coromandel, Ceylon, and Bengal, thence to China, but instead he stayed eighteen months in Maldives and became the chief judge.

Difficult to reach because of the rough anchorage, for centuries the island of Landhoo in Noonu Atoll (South Miladhummadulu Atoll) has been a stone-building and carving centre. Hidden among the banana plantations and coconut groves, the bush-covered remains of an ancient *hawitta* stand about six metres high. Known to the islanders as the *Maa Budhige* (temple), they recall that it was originally twice as high, enclosed by a square wall with steps that led up each side. Recently a statue was found inside the mound which would seem to be the remains of a Buddhist *stupa*.

But who built it? Possibly the Redin. These northern atolls are rich with stories and legends about these strange, mythical folk who first arrived it seems at Ihavandhoo, the most northerly of all the islands of Maldives. From there, they sailed down south to Landhoo. They moved so swiftly that it is claimed that they cooked their food on Landhoo and then sailed far south to Gan (Gamu) in Laamu Atoll to eat it.

Large heaps of big shells on Nalandhoo, a cluster of uninhabited islands, are said to be leftovers from the feast of the Redin who seem to be the Maldivian equivalent of those European giants with seven-league boots. But whoever the Redin were, they may well have left the masked dances still performed in the north in which words from a forgotten language are used to summon supernatural beings.

Ugoofaaru, the capital, is reputed to have the greatest number of fishermen of all the atolls and as a result Raa Atoll has become famous for its boat builders. The craftsmen on Innamaadhoo and Iguraidhoo are

unsurpassed for skills and design: even today most boats in Maldives are fashioned by primitive tools without a plan. All depends on the eye and experience of the chief carpenter.

The basic design and method of construction of the *dhoani*, like its cousin the Arab dhow, has changed little over the centuries. The carvel-built hull is made from the trunk of the coconut tree, with shark oil painted on as a preservative. Although modern naval architecture has confirmed the efficiency and seaworthiness of the ancient *dhoani* hull, change is slowly taking place.

The major one is in the method of construction. Traditional boat builders in Maldives build the hull first and add the frame later. At the new Alifushi Boat Yard the keel is laid first, the frame and stern added, and then the planks. The yard produces twenty or more large fishing boats a year. Since the fishermen now prefer engine to sail, the naval architect at the yard has made slight modifications to the traditional design and streamlined the hull. To enhance safety, two watertight bulkheads have been introduced.

Imported hardwoods from Malaysia are used to produce stronger and

Above: These boys on Kulhudhuffushi Island will probably spend more of their life at sea than on land, but there is still time for fun and games when their fathers' boats are in harbour.

Above: Fine examples of Maldivian lacquerware — lielaa jehun *— made on Thulhaadhoo Island in Baa Atoll. Turned on hand lathes, the vases and boxes are rubbed with yellow, red, and black resin imported from India before the intricate floral designs are carved by a sharp knife.*

more seaworthy vessels. Copper rivets nail the planks to the frame, and these are caulked with red oxide and cotton to make them watertight. On the outside, the hull is varnished with linseed oil and on the inside with coconut oil.

Even in the tropical climate and reef-strewn sea of Maldives, the boats should last at least twenty years. Yet, however precise the planking and caulking, the boats take so much water that the bilges have to be constantly pumped dry by hand.

Normally the buyer of a fishing *dhoani*, which can take up to two years to complete, pays the builders by instalment as the work progresses. But the process is often erratic — when the owner defaults on a payment, the carpenters drop tools. In the new boatyard, however, the shipbuilders work a twelve-hour day for a fixed wage and the future owners guarantee payment. In this way their boats will be finished within three or four months.

Extremely conservative, Maldivian fishermen have retained the basic design of their craft for centuries. Only in the last fifteen years have they recognized the advantage of engine over sail — and had the money to pay for one. But they see no reason to replace the original engine with an improved later model. Such an attitude has its advantages, for island blacksmiths using primitive techniques have learned to fashion spare parts for such engines. Invariably, the *dhoanis* carry a sail in case the engine breaks down or the wind is particularly good and they can save fuel.

Aboard the *dhoani*, the helmsman steers with a large tiller held between his legs. In rough weather, he has to hang on to the crutch that holds the yard when the sail is not in use — like riding a bucking bronco.

To become a captain (*keolhu*) requires intimate knowledge of the reefs and atoll entrances. Some *dhoanis* now carry compasses, but usually the *keolhu* steers by dead reckoning or by the island landmarks on the horizon. On approaching an island, a member of the crew goes forward as a lookout to direct him through the narrow channels of the reef. One small mistake can ground the *dhoani* on the reef.

Even when there is a bunk below, the crew prefer to sleep on a mat on deck under the stars. Comfort is less important than a sense of freedom and it is safer on deck when a sudden squall blows up or the anchor slips.

When the wind blows from the right direction, even *dhoanis* with engines set the sail they always carry. The captain calls all hands on deck, including the cook, to hoist the long yard pole which carries the sail. 'Aa-haa-a-a-haa-a', goes the cry as they heave on the rough rope. As the yard reaches the top of the mast, the sail billows out in the breeze — like the white wing of a magnificent bird. Now the *dhoani* leans over and cuts merrily through the waves as the sheet is pulled in and made fast astern.

All is transformed. The dull thud and shudder of the engine give way to the creaking of the rigging and the splash and dash of water rushing past the sleek hull. Nothing compares to the peace and beauty of sail — or its efficiency: canvas and wood are in harmony with wind and water, leaving no waste or pollution. Visibly affected by the change of tempo

and movement, the crew gather peacefully on the cool foredeck in the shade of the billowing sail — just as their forefathers before them.

However, the euphoric mood can change unexpectedly. Squalls appear from nowhere and the sky grows dark as the stiffening wind whips up the white-flecked waves. Suddenly, the *dhoani* lunges, its rigging and sails straining taut. In the galley, pots and pans go crashing to the deck. Whipped off their line, drying clothes disappear in the wake. And spray crashing over the prow is carried by the wind into the face of the anxious helmsman. Slacking off the sail, he turns his vessel bow on into the mounting sea.

Some captains make for the middle of the squall. If lucky, by some strange climatic quirk of this area of the Indian Ocean, it will divide into two separate storms. Sailing past the brooding, distended clouds on either side the *dhoani* once again reaches calm seas, clear skies, and blazing sun.

Sometimes there is no escape and they must weather the storm, leaving all in the hands of Allah who decides everything. As an added precaution, they may try to appease the spirits of the deep with rites and

Above: Gripping action in the finals of the annual inter-atoll football competition. After the game, the hosts on Eydhafushi Island put on a large street dinner for the guest team and its supporters. The drums are then brought out for a party which continues into the early hours.

Above: Ripening breadfruit provides starchy food as well as welcome shade.

offerings. In the final outcome, they depend on the tried and tested design of their boat. After all, the men who built it are their friends and neighbours.

The northernmost extremities of Maldives consists of virtually a single chain of more than 200 islands 140 kilometres long. For administrative purposes they are divided into four groups: Noonu, Shaviyani, Haa Dhaalu (South Thiladhunmathee), and Haa Alifu (North Thiladhunmathee).

With its capital of Manadhoo, Noonu, the most southerly atoll, may soon be brought into the tourist orbit. Certainly, its desert islands and unsurpassed marine life have vast potential.

Apart from fish, nearly all food is imported, although bananas, breadfruit, and papayas provide shade and, where possible, families grow chillies, pumpkins, and yams in their small gardens. Finger millet (*bimbi*) is also grown, then ground to powder with wooden pestles to produce a nutritious porridge for babies and young children.

Most locally caught tuna goes to the canning factory, but few islanders now bother to dry fish except for their own consumption and export to the neighbouring islands. The traditional process is long and laborious. Gutted and beheaded, the fish are boiled in fresh water for fifteen minutes, then smoked over charcoal for twenty-four hours in a small kitchen, after which they are laid out in the sun for four days.

In the tropics, such cured fish was widely sought after in the days when there was no refrigeration. As tough as leather, the hard dried lumps of tuna meat last for years. Sri Lankans used it as a condiment, scraping small fragments into their curries. Nowadays, after gutting, the fish is salted and packed in containers for two or three days and then sun dried on wooden tables by the beach until crisp and bone-dry.

North of Raa Atoll, and west of Noonu Atoll, the lagoon of Shaviyani Atoll is deep enough to allow the easy passage of boats. The atoll has a stormy history. Many of its islands have been devastated in the last two centuries by raging storms — on 7 May 1812; 21 January 1821; and again on 9 January 1955. Some also suffer occasional earth tremors.

Originally, the citizens of Funadhoo (also known as Farukolhufunadhoo), the capital, migrated from Bomasdhoo in Noonu Atoll because of Funadhoo's fine harbour, a deep inlet that fills and empties with the tide. In a land which knows neither river nor mountain, the creek is called *koaru*, the nearest *Dhivehi* word for 'river'.

Most island populations shift as a result of disease or death. Traditionally, if fewer than forty men are able to muster for Friday prayers, the population moves to a more populous island. Funadhoo Island, however, has long been inhabited for as well as the ruins of a mosque, the large cemetery nearby dates back many centuries. An old tombstone is dedicated to the 'memory of Ibrahim son of Funadhoo Marudhuru who died on Sunday 11, Zul-Gaidha, 1238 AH'.

Unfortunately, as in the south, the art of carving tombstones has virtually died out. Since it involved much hard work for little pay, apprentices could not be found. The old stone-carvers simply gave up. On Landhoo, the only stone-carver has now retired; and with him a unique art with an ancient tradition.

Sailing north through the atoll you come to Magoodhoo, a beautiful

Above: New centre in memory of Muhammad Thakurufaanu on the island of Utheemu in Haa Alifu Atoll, the birthplace of the national hero who figured prominently in the country's fight to regain independence.

island with an industrious population and a wide, grass-covered pathway from the landing spot. Although beautiful to behold, this carpet of green demonstrates the dangers facing Maldives as a result of the rise in sea-level. While Magoodhoo is surrounded by white coral beaches two metres above sea-level, the centre of the island is sinking. Indeed, the water table is now so high that there is a rapidly expanding freshwater lake. During the rains the foundations of houses are underwater and their coral walls are collapsing due to subsidence. Islanders constantly bring barrowloads of coral sand from the beaches to spread on the floors of their houses and the surrounding area to keep their feet dry.

The nearby island of Maakadoodhoo has the largest population in the atoll and is known for its *fathuli hakuru*. The Maldivian answer to jaggery — a coarse brown sugar — *fathuli hakuru* is made from coconut palm sap or toddy.

Lying north of Shaviyani Atoll, the seventy-seven islands that form South and North Thiladhunmathee were split into the administrative districts of Haa Dhaalu Atoll and Haa Alifu Atoll in 1958. Although

Above: Interior of Muhammad Thakurufaanu's palace on Utheemu Island. The white flags are left as a sign of respect, and the floor is strewn with very fine white sand.

Haa Dhaalu is contiguous to Shaviyani Atoll, the northern extremity of Haa Alifu forms its own separate, smaller atoll.

The area is noted for making coir rope from the fibres of the coconut, which for Maldivians is the 'tree of life', as essential as fish to the islanders' livelihood. The ubiquitous coconut provides virtually everything needed for survival: milk for drinking and cooking; flesh for curries and cakes; fibres for coir and rope; sap for 'toddy', or syrup; fronds for roofs, mats, and walls; trunks for boats and houses; and waste for firewood.

Long ago Ibn Battuta noted that the coconut is one of the strangest and most useful of trees:

The nut resembles a man's head, for it has marks like eyes and a mouth, and the contents, when it is green, are like the brain. It has fibres like hair. . . . Amongst its properties are that it strengthens the body, fattens, and adds redness to the face.

Certainly, anyone lucky enough to open a young, green coconut will never forget its deliciously fresh, sweet juice. After draining the nut you can split it open and scrape out the soft pulp with a piece of rind. Nothing could be more refreshing after a midday landing on a remote island. However tiring the journey, you feel instantly invigorated and ready to explore and investigate.

The method of collecting toddy has remained unchanged for centuries. Cutting the stalk on which the fruit grows in the crown of the palm, the toddy-tapper places a small bowl beneath the cut to collect the oozing sap. If this is done in the morning, the bowl is full by evening and another bowl may be tied further along the stalk. Simmered for a long time, the sap becomes a delicious, sweet syrup. Exported in the past to India, Yemen, and China, nowadays whatever is not consumed locally is sent to the market in Malé.

Coconut oil is extracted by peeling the ripe nuts, leaving them to dry in the sun, then boiling them. The oil is used for cooking, lighting, and as a hair dressing.

Coir is made from the hairy husk of the coconut after it has been soaked for about three months or so in watery pits by the seashore. The husk is then beaten to release the fibre, which the women spin by hand and roll into thin string on their thighs. In turn, these are woven to make strong, floating anchor and mooring ropes. Maldivian coir ropes were once widely exported but these days there is little demand.

Dredgers regularly clear the approach channel to the modern harbour of Kulhudhuffushi, capital of Haa Dhaalu Atoll. With a population of more than 4,500, and a large school and regional hospital, it is one of the largest towns in Maldives. More than half of the menfolk go to sea on ocean-going vessels or work in the tourist resorts. Those that remain are famous shark fishermen. Laden down with *cadjan* and coir made by the women from the atoll, large *dhoanis* sustain a lively trade with Malé.

The twenty-five-kilometre-long reef at the south-west extremity is a major shipping hazard, the site of many wrecks. The *Persia Merchant* went down on the tip of the western side in August 1658, but the worst toll was that taken in the nineteenth century when the *Hayston* (1819),

the *Royal Family* (19 August 1868), and the *George Reid* (26 September 1872) all came to grief.

Doubtless, the ships were swept to their graves by the sudden storms that erupt in the area during the south-west monsoon. Scuba divers should note the intriguing salvage to be recovered from these waters. For the richness and shape of their coral and the staggering variety of marine life, the reefs are certainly as good as anywhere in the Indian Ocean.

Another interesting feature of this atoll is Faridhoo Island — the highest in the archipelago — although you may find it hard to tell. It is all of three metres above sea-level, though verifying this fact is a challenge as landing on the island is difficult.

The island of Kumundhoo is noted for its toddy-tapping and two unexplored ruins with circular foundations on its eastern side. Budding explorers should be aware that they need special permission from the government to excavate these ancient ruins. The amount of priceless and irreplaceable dressed megalithic stone locked away in recent island walls scarcely bears thinking about.

The most northerly reach of Maldives is known as Haa Alifu Atoll

Above: Singing in chorus and working themselves up into a frenzy, bodu beru *drummers beat out rhythms brought from Africa centuries ago. The drums are made from hollowed coconut trunks, covered in skin from manta rays or the stomach of sharks, and held together by coir.*

Above: Although traditionally women's percussion did not extend much beyond tapping out the rhythm on water pots, on Huvarafushi Island in the most northerly part of Haa Alifu Atoll they have recently taken to playing the bodu beru *drums and singing in time with them.*

although this is somewhat misleading. In fact, Dhidhdhoo, the capital, with its ideal anchorage for yachts cruising through this part of the Indian Ocean, is part of the long atoll that makes up Noonu, Shaviyani, and Haa Dhaalu.

The beautiful island of Utheemu nearby is something of a national shrine, the birthplace of Muhammad Thakurufaanu, the national hero. It can only be reached by landing from small boats. When the south-west monsoon is blowing even these are often swamped by surf.

Many visitors brave the peril, however, to pay homage to the 'father' of the nation whose wooden 'palace' has been renovated. Although the original thatched roof has been replaced by tiles, it evokes more than any other existing building in Maldives what life was like for wealthy Maldivians all those centuries ago.

You have to stoop your head to enter. Strewn with the finest of white coral sand, the floor is a refinement of great beauty. The small rooms contain fine wooden chests, precious lacquerware, and small, ornamental beds.

The lintel of the doorway was placed low, so the story goes, to prevent

the dead from walking out — if they left the house before being buried and walked down to the beach, they could come back and eat up all the living.

Guests and dignitaries were received in the large separate building nearby, where the floors are covered with woven mats and the walls with beautiful cotton drapes that have colourful abstract designs.

Well-remembered for his local connections, Muhammad Thakurufaanu's first wife was a girl from a poor family on neighbouring Baarah Island. She served as a maid to the wife of Sultan Ali, who was killed by the Portuguese. As Muhammad Thakurufaanu's exploits made him famous, Ali's daughter fell in love with him as soon as they met; she became his second wife. Although from such different backgrounds, by all accounts, the two wives got on well. Thakurufaanu's common touch and such stories of royal love endear him still to the minds and hearts of Maldivians.

The nearby mosque, which points west towards the setting sun, and not to Mecca, is almost four and a half centuries old. Buried in the adjoining stone mausoleum is the body of Thakurufaanu's father. As

*Above: Delights of island cuisine: rice and fish curry cooked in coconut milk, highly seasoned omelette with chillies, spicy side-dishes of onion and lime and finely cut fresh greens. The varied savouries (*kuli eche*) are usually based on a mixture of smoked tuna, grated coconut, lime juice, onion, and chilli, often rolled in balls or covered in thin pastry. The sweets (*foni eche*) are principally made from flour, sugar, and eggs liberally mixed with spices and shaped into mouth-watering shapes, along with very sweet custard (*kastaad*). And then there are pomegranates, mangoes, and bananas picked fresh from the surrounding trees, all washed down with rosewater and hot sweet tea.*

Above: Dusky-eyed youngster who may spend her entire life on the same remote island.

a sign of respect, the mausoleum is constantly decorated with white flags that flap in the sea breeze.

The beautiful well by the mosque is made out of one stone which, according to local legend, arrived on the island through divine providence. The story goes that the Thakurufaanu brothers collected the stone from Seenu Atoll in the south, but when they were caught in a storm in the One-and-Half-Degree Channel they threw it overboard to lighten their vessel. Miraculously, instead of sinking swiftly a thousand fathoms or more to Davy Jones' Locker it was washed ashore on Utheemu, at the other end of the Maldivian archipelago. Such are the stories that gather round heroes.

Another legend relates that when Muhammad Thakurufaanu placed two stakes from trees brought from Baarah near the beach in order to make sails, the stakes took root. One tree still stands — nearly 400 years old.

Surrounded by lovely gardens, the recently built Bodu Thakurufaanu Memorial Centre has a library and conference rooms and the 600 or so inhabitants of this remote northern island are now accustomed to receiving important guests from Malé. More than once, President Gayoom and his ministers have made the pilgrimage there to celebrate Independence Day and pay homage to the national hero.

Another overgrown monument to a bygone era, on Kelai Island at the extreme north-eastern tip of the atoll, is the ruin of the British base built during the Second World War. It is the northern counterpart of Gan at the other end of the Maldives archipelago.

The most northerly true atoll is Ihavandhippolhu, although it is now part of the Haa Alifu administrative atoll. It is reached by crossing Gallandhoo Kadu, the five-kilometre-wide channel in which the tidal stream sets east, north-east with the flood and west, south-west with the ebb.

Its most important island, Huvarafushi, has a population of 2,000, but like many Maldivian islands it is so small that from the crossroads in the centre of the village you can see the sea in all four directions. Fishing is poor this far north and there are few coconuts for coir making. Yet this remote speck in the Indian Ocean is the commercial centre of the atoll, with a new school built by the Japanese.

In the school library you come across such varied books as *Pious Caliphs*, Ruskin's *Elements of Drawing*, *Principles of Biochemistry*, and *Practical Human Relations* — all part of the modern intellectual melting pot of Maldives. Yet while Western influence is reaching the country, particularly in the form of technology and science, the culture remains fundamentally Islamic. It will be a long time before island traditions undergo drastic change.

Renowned for their music and dancing, the women of Huvarafushi regularly perform the traditional *bandiya jehun*, swinging their heads and shoulders in a line as they tap out a rhythm on metal water pots (*bandia*). It would seem to be a kind of harvest dance, similar to those of southern India. Nowadays, the women also play the *bodu beru* drums, chanting away as one of their number dances enticingly in an Arabic fashion.

The northernmost island of Maldives, Thuraakunu, is inhabited but difficult to reach as there is a strong swell outside the reef and no lagoon.

Opposite: No island is complete without its resident heron, patient sentinel guarding the channel through the coral reef.

Above: Sundown over Kuda Bandos, a glowing tribute to one more memorable day in Maldives.

Although this is land's end as far as Maldives is concerned, 290 kilometres north lies Minicoy, the southern part of the Indian state of Lakshadweep (formerly known as Laccadive) Islands, where they still speak a *Dhivehi* dialect called *Mahl*. In the eleventh century an Arab geographer split the archipelago into the Maldives and the Laccadives, but local fishermen made no such arbitrary distinctions.

The ties between the two peoples are strong despite the ever-deepening void beneath your keel as you sail on northward at the end of your *Journey through Maldives*.

6. Over the Blue Edge

More of Maldives, of course, is under water than above. It has the perfect ingredients to make it one of the great diving centres of the world: desert islands, clear waters, thriving coral reefs, and a huge variety of marine life. With its wonderfully warm turquoise lagoons and magnificent coral drop-offs, Maldives is one of the most ideal places on earth to go beneath the water and appreciate the beauties of this quiet and slow-moving world.

The most striking impression is the sheer number and variety of fish, all with beautiful patterns and marvellous colours. There are well over 1,000 species of fish, more than half of which can regularly be seen swimming on the reefs.

At first, you can easily be overwhelmed by the swirling confusion of fish but with careful observation you will soon begin to spot the different species: the groupers, fusiliers, sweetlips, butterfly, angel, surgeon, parrot, and puffer fish. Then there are unforgettable encounters with sharks, manta rays, and moray eels.

It takes longer to appreciate the different species of coral, but it is equally worth the effort. Maldives is one of the richest coral areas in the world, comparable only to the Philippines and Australia's Great Barrier Reef. There are as many as 200 different species of hard coral alone. But it is the shapes which they form that make it so amazing: caverns, fans, shafts, canyons, and boulders. They create a kaleidoscope of colour in the clear, sunlit water.

It is so beautiful underwater that at first it is difficult to know where to look. It is very easy to drift or flip from patch to patch on the reef, looking for evermore breathtaking shapes and colours. But if you want to unlock its secrets, you have to stay a while in one place. To travel fast over the reef is equivalent to flying over the Amazon forest instead of walking through it.

You do not have to be a professional diver to appreciate this underwater world. All you need is a bit of rubber and glass to stop your eyes from smarting from the saltwater, and the ability to swim. Maldives is the perfect place to begin snorkeling, mask on face, fins on feet, and air tube in mouth. By these simple appliances, you become an honorary fish in the magical world below the surface.

What you will find is simply mind-blowing — like being in a brightly lit aquarium full of the most exotic tropical fish. And the experience is guaranteed to be the same every time you dip your head below the water.

In the Indian Ocean, however, there are no glass walls. Apart from the marine life, there is the sheer delight of floating in warm and buoyant water, where every move is effortless. To wallow in the shallow lagoon with warm sun on your back and white coral sand below is one of the most calming experiences in the world.

Swimming through a channel in the coral reef for the first time is something else, literally breathtaking, like suddenly going over an abyss in a dream. The coral edge drops away to the blue unknown, but instead of hurtling forever downwards you drift and glide like an aeroplane.

Resist the impulse to return to the shallows of the lagoon for you are perfectly safe, even though lurking deep down by the coral face there are the dark, sinister shapes of big fish and sharks.

Previous pages: One of the countless desert islands waiting to be discovered in Maldives — countless not only because some are difficult to define but because they come and go with the constant movement of wind and sea.

*Opposite: Two schooling bannerfish (*Heniochus diphreutes*) taking off on their own for a friendly jaunt. Feeding on plankton, they usually live in open water off the reef edge. Their adult size is about fifteen centimetres.*

The water temperature around Maldives is like a warm bath: a constant 20°–30° centigrade (68°–86°F) year-round. In the lagoons it often reaches 32° centigrade (90°F). The calmest seas and clearest skies are from November to May, when the winds are north-easterly. At this time the currents outside the atolls run east to west at an average of twenty-four metres a minute.

The roughest seas are during June, and sometimes October or early November, when strong winds blow from the south-west. Running from west to east, during this period the currents reach thirty metres a minute.

The clearest underwater visibility is from March to April, towards the end of the north-east monsoon when forty metres is normal. On some occasions it is possible to see seventy metres down the coral edge. In April plankton begins to bloom, reducing visibility to about twenty metres. But on the eastern side of the atolls this can be the most interesting time, for the plankton-rich upwellings attract manta rays and whale sharks.

Once underwater, of course, it makes little difference what it is like on top, although travelling to and from the dive site in a rolling *dhoani* makes some divers seasick.

Whatever the season, local visibility is also affected by the rise and fall of the tide. The incoming tide brings clear water, while the falling tide is richer in plankton and sediments.

The Maldive islands are simply the tips of the great submerged mountain range that stretches from the Lakshadweep Islands to the Chagos Islands. They are tiny parts of the coral reefs that have burst through the surface of the sea but which are in constant danger of being submerged again. Whatever happens to the people who have managed to scratch a living for a few thousand years on these specks of sand above the water, the life of the ocean deep will continue as it has done for aeons.

It seems likely that at one time the peaks of the mountain chain may have been well above the water as large islands. Coral then probably grew around them as fringing reefs and over millions of years the islands subsided — due to a combination of erosion, settling of the sea-bed, and rising sea-level. What was eventually left was a ring of coral near the surface of the water — the rim of today's atolls.

Although its shape may vary, each island follows a basic pattern. The green vegetation above the water in the centre gives way to the white coral sand of the beach. A band of shallow water follows in the lagoon between the beach and the outer reef, the white sandy bottom of which turns the water a bright turquoise. This gives way to a shallow platform of coral reef known as the reef flat which may dry out at low tides. At the reef edge, the reef slope suddenly drops away.

On the inside of the atoll the sandy floor is only about fifty metres deep, but on the seaward side it drops down more than a thousand fathoms. Descending the outer reef, there is often a sloping terrace of about ten metres, a steep escarpment to about fifty metres, then a sloping fore-reef to ninety metres, before the vertical drop to the ocean floor.

These reefs are made of an infinite number of corals. For long, corals were thought to be plants because of their similarity to flowers, but in fact they are simple animals in polyp form. They belong to the same class

Above: Hawksbill turtle, clumsy on land but wonderfully agile in the water. Maldives was once famous for its turtles, but the islanders' taste for its flesh and eggs, and the visitors' desire for tortoiseshell jewellery, have seriously threatened its numbers. Between June and November, a turtle can return three or four times to lay up to a thousand eggs in excavated pits on the same beach; the young hatch at night and then have to make the perilous journey down to the sea. Some divers in Maldives claim to have developed intimate relationships with turtles, taking rides on their backs and being followed in turn. Hawksbills can easily swim at twenty-five kilometres an hour.

as anemones and jellyfish, and vary from under one millimetre to several centimetres in size, normally shaped like a cylinder with a central mouth that has a ring of poisonous tentacles.

With the latter, the corals sweep passing microscopic animals into their bodies. In a remarkable example of symbiosis, many also feed on organic compounds leaked by algae living within their tissues. Although some colours come from the corals themselves, the spectacular reds, greens, yellows, and browns that turn the reef into a kaleidoscope of colour are produced by the algae living within them.

The 200 or so species of coral in Maldives are influenced by the intensity of the sunlight and the strength of the underwater swell; they tend to be small and delicate in the sandy lagoons, while large and robust on the reef edge.

Varied in colour, corals can be both hard and soft. The beautiful soft ones lack an external skeleton. They are fleshy or water-filled, strengthened by numerous 'spicules' in their walls. Although biologically more primitive than their harder cousins they far surpass them in the brilliance of their colours. The hard stony corals which build the reef only live in a narrow zone of warm, clear, sunlit water. During the day corals close up and all that you can see are the hard skeletons and algae living within. Only when they feed at night do they open up and extend their tentacles.

There is great competition on the reef for space between the hard and soft corals. Soft corals emit poison, while hard corals sting with their tentacles; a thin divide on the reef often marks the battle line between the two types.

From one tiny polyp, mighty things can grow. Since it can reproduce sexually and asexually, one polyp alone can begin the construction of a reef. Countless must follow over millions of years, however, building on the limestone skeletons of their ancestors. Deposits of calcium-producing algae and encrusting sponges complete the job by solidifying the whole to create one of the most productive and beautiful environments on this planet.

Depending on the sunlight and wave energy, these tiny creatures create structures of such size, strength, shape, and beauty that no human architect can equal them. Fans, leaves, columns, arches, and caves are only a fraction of the forms they can take. The very scale and grandeur of a coral reef defies the imagination.

Although they build massive structures, only the top in the sunlit water is alive. The growth rate of coral is also very slow, averaging between about one centimetre and a maximum of ten centimetres a year. They are also extremely delicate. Corals easily come under stress due to lack of sunlight, lowered salinity, increased temperature, and above all pollution. When this happens the coral becomes bleached as the coral polyps expel the symbiotic algae from their tissues.

If a swimmer breaks off a piece of coral by walking or holding onto the reef, he can also kill part of the colony. Even touching the living coral removes a slimy mucus which protects them from infection and falling sediment. The white featureless desert of dead coral near some of the most popular diving sites is a tragic sight.

The reef, of course, can extract its own vengeance. Fire coral, a feathery hydroid that secretes a stony skeleton, often gives a painful sting. Many anemones and jellyfish do not encourage close contact. Sea urchins have sharp spines that can even pierce a wet suit. But the most dangerous invertebrate is the *conus* family, a shell that can instantly poison a fish with its proboscis.

Maldivian reefs are teeming with countless other creatures. There are as many as 5,000 different species of molluscs. Most shells tend to be active at night and rest during the day. Cowries, of course, are the most famous, since they were used as money for centuries by the countries adjoining the Indian Ocean.

The special lustre on their colourful and neat shapes comes from the minute chalk algae exuded by their mantles. Cowries usually live in shallow water. The most impressive shell is undoubtedly the giant triton, which feeds on starfish and crustacea. It can grow to almost half a metre, and the shell is still used on some islands as a horn to call villagers to a meeting. While cowries and nautical shells are abundant, conch, pearl, and trident shells are rare, though still available in tourist shops.

In this wonderful underwater world, marine life has evolved to create

Following pages: Sweetlips fish (Gaterin sp.) *find safety in numbers by schooling, since many eyes are better than one and moving together reduces energy output. When attacked by a predator, the school can move with great speed and agility, with each fish orientating itself by a sensory lateral line that runs down the length of its body.*

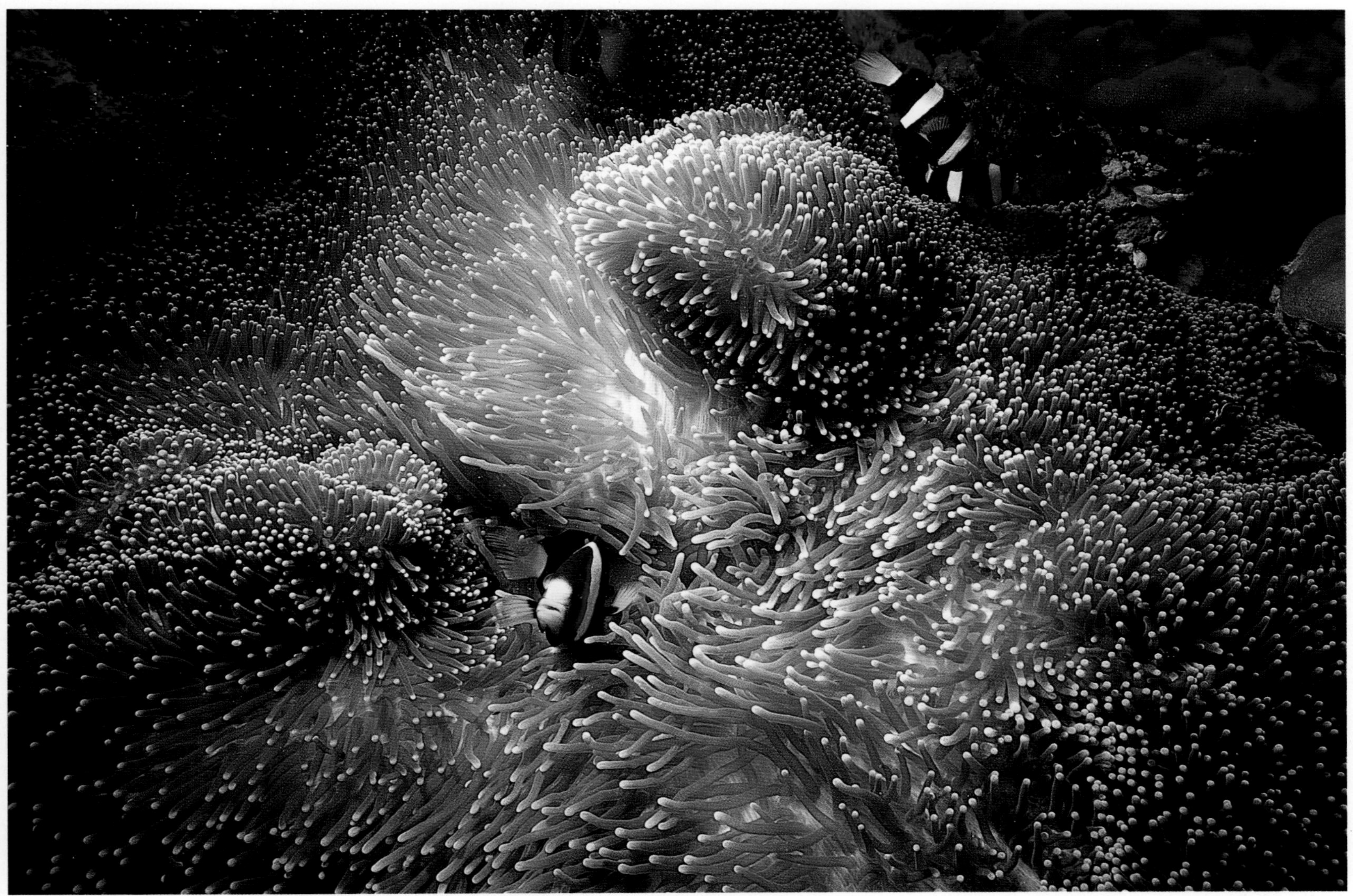

Above: Symbiosis on the reef edge: Clark's anemone fish (Amphiprion clarkii) *living amongst the stinging tentacles of giant sea anemones. Such omnivorous fish have developed a layer of mucus on their bodies to immunize themselves against the anemones' tentacles which act like protective arms around them. In turn, the fish leave scraps of food for their host and can frighten away potential predators like butterflyfish. The adult size of Clark's anemone fish is fifteen centimetres.*

a remarkable equilibrium. While all species live off each other, there are many different types of symbiotic relationships. Some, like the little bugs or isopods which live on fish, or the remora fish which attaches itself to sharks and rays, are parasitical. Others are more commensal, as with the pilot fish which saves energy by riding the shark's bow wave and picking up its scraps.

An interesting example of symbiosis and mutual benefit is the clown fish which lives among the tentacles of the giant anemone. While poisonous to other fish, the tentacles act like protective arms for the clown fish. In return, the fish feeds its host scraps of food and attacks marauding creatures. In Maldives, clown fish are called soap fish (*saiboani mas*), referring to the slimy covering that probably protects them from being stung by the tentacles of the anemones.

Cleaning is another mutually beneficial habit developed by certain fishes and shrimps. One prime example is the bright, blue-striped cleaner wrasse which lives by picking parasites, dead skin, and scales from larger fish. Two or three of them will often position themselves on coral outcrops along the upper reef slope waiting for customers to come to

Above: Two spotted groupers with thick lips and strong teeth.

their 'cleaning stations'. Groupers, eels, and barracuda which could easily snap them up as tasty morsels allow them to forage in their open mouths. Divers may even find one trying to clean their ears.

The most important example of symbiosis in the reef, however, is that between algae and the hard corals. Algae live in a protected environment and use the waste products of the polyp, while in return they produce oxygen and nutrient compounds for the coral. Coral can exist without algae, but not well enough to grow into huge atolls and great barrier reefs.

Coral reefs are among the most productive ecosystems in the sea. But while they produce a great deal of organic matter, surprisingly enough there are very few visible green plants. This is because most of the plant material exists in the form of tiny algae that live within the tissues of the coral itself and enable it to form its limestone casing. Since they rely on sunlight to grow by photosynthesis, the reef-forming corals are confined to shallow waters.

Darting forever in and out of the beautiful corals the reef fish of the Maldives are divided into herbivores and carnivores. Although seaweeds

*Following pages: The most common shark in Maldives — the white-tip reef shark (*Triaenodon obesus*) — gives divers the beady eye. Scavengers and predators, sharks can pick up the smell of blood several kilometres downcurrent, but given the abundance of marine life in Maldives they are generally friendly to humans. The white-tip reef shark grows up to two metres long and lives on the reef slope.*

grow fast on the reefs in the warm waters of the Indian Ocean, they are immediately cropped back by the herbivorous fish.

The most common and fascinating are the parrotfish, so called because of their beaks, bright colours, and 'flapping' way of swimming. There are about thirty species of parrotfish in Maldives. While scraping off thin layers of algae and other organic matter they take in large amounts of coral rock which is then ground down by powerful sets of teeth. After digesting the organic material, they then excrete puffs of coral sand — the main building block of the islands of Maldives. Another feature that they share with many other fish is their ability to change sex as they grow older.

Another conspicuous herbivore is the surgeonfish with its scalpel-like blades on either side of its tail. Although they may seem destructive, the herbivores do a useful job by breaking down plant material for other creatures. They also prevent the reef from becoming overgrown with plants that would cut out the sunlight and check the growth of the corals.

Most reef fish are carnivorous, or at least omnivorous. One group of specialized carnivores is the butterflyfish that feeds on small animals, including coral polyps, on the reef edge and slope and have perfectly adapted snouts and teeth for the task. The smaller and more solitary angelfish, on the other hand, feeds mainly on sponges.

Broadly speaking, the carnivores of the Maldivian reefs may be divided into plankton eaters and lurking or roving predators.

Plankton consists of minute plants and animals that float in open water. During the day these are not visible to the naked eye, but at night they can sometimes be seen shining phosphorescent in the wake of a boat or a dolphin. Some of the most common fish living off plankton are the fusilier and the banner fish, which form large schools during the day in the open water. At night, they take refuge in holes in the reef when such nocturnal plankton-eaters as the batfish, large-eyed soldier, and squirrelfish become active.

By schooling, fish find safety in numbers. Many eyes are better than two in spotting would-be predators. Schooling also reduces the amount of energy needed for swimming. When a larger predatory fish attacks, they bunch together and move in the same direction with great precision, swirling around to create confusion. In order to be successful, the predator has to single out a particular fish and go for it. When attacking a school some predators hunt in groups for greater efficiency.

Fish orientate themselves by a sensory lateral line that runs the length of their body, enabling them to move with great dexterity and speed in the middle of a school without bumping into each other. They also have a ventral line along their underside that enables them to sense the nearest rocks; under the ceiling of a cave or overhang, they will often swim upside down with ease.

Plankton in the sea around Maldives increases during the south-west monsoon, when the water takes on a greyish haze as the wind blows the local waters eastwards and causes an upwelling of nutrient-rich deep water. The result is a bloom of plankton which is eaten by great schools of small fish.

This is the best time to see the large filter feeders like the manta rays which come up to the eerie waters of the eastern reefs. Ancient mariners

called them 'Devil Rays' because of their 'horns'; the graceful mantas well up like spectres from the mighty deep, gliding and hovering over the reef where they are groomed by innumerable cleaner fish. They can be up to four metres across. Their so-called 'horns' are used to scoop plankton into their wide mouths. Such an enormous creature dwarfs the frail diver. They appear gentle and caring, often lifting a wing over a diver's head in an apparent gesture of sympathy as they go by.

Another visitor from the deep is the whale shark, the biggest fish in the world. It too is a gentle giant, filter-feeding on plankton and small fish.

The 'lie-in-wait' predators are some of the most extraordinary and dangerous fish of all. They lurk motionless until a shrimp or fish passes by and then grab it with amazing speed. These include lizard, scorpion, lion, hawk, and stone fish — all names that reflect their appearance.

While waiting quietly to eat, some sedentary fellows like the stone and scorpion fish camouflage themselves so well to avoid being eaten that it is easy to mistake them for bits of coral. Which is not good news for divers and snorkelers, for they have developed a row of poisonous spines along their backs that cause severe pain. Stone fish release the strongest poison of all fish. While the scorpion fish would seem to be camouflaged in order to improve chances of catching prey, the lionfish is brightly coloured, no doubt to warn off any would-be predator by advertising its poisonous spines.

Another form of protection, as in the case of the poisonous puffer fish, is to inflate the body with large quantities of water when threatened. This defence is also practised by porcupine fish that, as their name suggests, have the additional defence of many spines all over their body.

One of the most graceful carnivores is the spotted eagle ray that glides effortlessly through the water, soaring along with a few slow flaps of its wings. It feeds on crustaceans and molluscs on the reef slope and in the atoll lagoons. Two or three reef stingrays can often be found lying on the sandy bottom of a cave in the coral slope; since they can lash out with the venomous spine at the base of their tails, they are best left alone.

Among the roving predator fish, the bluefin jack is a fierce customer. They usually hunt in small groups along the reef slope, but they sometimes dash into the lagoon after a shoal of small fish which in their frenzy to escape sometimes beach themselves.

Moray eels are usually considered very dangerous. They can reach up to a metre and a half, and as they open their mouths to breathe in and out, they reveal sharp, inward-pointing teeth. Yet in Maldives they often seem quite tame. Diving instructors get to know their daytime hideaways in the reef and stroke their soft slimy necks; they sway their heads in sensual pleasure and slowly their bodies emerge from the crevice in which they hide.

Nevertheless, you should not put your hand in their lair; their apparent calm can be deceptive. At night they come out and look for prey. Their sense of smell is well-developed, and they scavenge as well as take fish. Maldivian fishermen hate to catch a moray eel on their hooks, for with their powerful body and strong teeth they can fight a long time at the bottom of a boat.

Barracuda also have a bad reputation. Certainly they have very nasty

Above: Countless golden silver sprat sweep through one of the many underwater coral gardens around Maldives.

Following pages: Holed up in the reef edge, a moray eel (Gymnothorax) *allows its soft, slimy neck to be stroked. Moray eels reach up to a metre and a half in length. With powerful bodies and sharp, inward-pointing teeth, they are usually considered extremely dangerous and Maldivian fishermen hate to hook these ferocious fighters. At night they leave their dens to hunt for fish along the reef.*

teeth and are very curious. But they seldom attack in clear water — unless perhaps swimmers who wear bright jewellery or flash the white soles of their feet, which might be mistaken for tasty morsels.

The most spectacular predator, and the one that many come to see in Maldives, is the shark. As a scavenger and a hunter, it has an extremely strong sense of smell and can pick up the scent of blood many kilometres downstream. Its hearing is also acute. But it cannot see well, usually living in the dim light of a world eighty metres deep.

To see a shark go into attack is an awesome sight. It is a creature of great power and grace but, unlike the dolphin, it seems to have little desire to play or to communicate. They are such fierce and voracious predators that they become frenetic with the smell and taste of blood; when injured they have been known to snap at their own trailing entrails.

Nearly all human beings have a primordial fear of being dragged underwater by some terrifying creature from the deep — a fear used to good effect by Jules Verne in *Twenty Thousand Leagues Under the Sea*, but with mischievous results in films like *Jaws*.

Sharks have been associated with all manner of deep psychological fears about predators and drowning. Yet these fearless creatures have been maligned, whatever their symbolic significance in the unconscious might be. Only the great whites, which have sea mammals as a large part of their diet, are potentially dangerous. The sharks in Maldives are especially friendly; after an initial shock you soon become accustomed to them swimming by. They are rarely aggressive since their normal food supply is so abundant.

Like all sharks, however, the local ones are best left alone. They become aggressive if people splash about or corner them. If they go into an attack mode, swimming fast with nose lowered and pectoral fins sharply down, the best thing to do is to back off slowly and calmly — to flee only triggers their hunting instinct. Some divers advise hitting them on the nose with something hard, getting them to bite on a plastic fin rather than a tasty arm, and as a last resort to gouge out their eyes with a thumb (although to have the *sang-froid* to do this while being chewed seems highly unlikely).

In Maldives the most common sharks are the white-tip reef and the smaller nurse shark. They only become aggressive when teased and tormented. The grey reef shark does not grow much bigger than two metres but they come in shoals of a dozen or more; they are the ones that the intrepid divemasters of Maldives used to feed mouth-to-mouth. The beautiful silver-tip makes a rarer and more memorable appearance, although the whale shark, the largest fish in the world, is fairly common on the easterly coral reefs during the south-west monsoon.

Maldives was once famous for its turtles, especially the hawksbill turtle, which is omnivorous, eating almost anything including coral. Hawksbills easily swim at twenty-five kilometres an hour; the giant leatherback turtle reaches speeds of more than thirty-five kilometres an hour.

Unfortunately, the local taste for turtle omelettes and flesh and the tourist fashion for tortoiseshell jewellery have led to a serious decline in their numbers, despite the fact that between the months of June and

November, a female turtle can return three or four times to lay up to 1,000 eggs in different excavated nests on the beach. Not only do the islanders take the eggs, but when the young hatch at night and make their way clumsily to the sea, they are easily picked off by predators. Steps have been taken, however, to control the human exploitation of turtles.

Unlike the turtle, dolphins are abundant in Maldives, and large schools are often seen leaping out of the water between the atolls. They frequently play along the edge of the reef. The most common is the bottlenose dolphin, which is dark grey and has a long, broad beak as its name implies. Feeding on fish and crustaceans, these mammals offer no danger to divers. However, where dolphins in other seas interact voluntarily with humans, in Maldives they tend to veer away when approached. They have not yet been tamed. Perhaps it is better that way.

For centuries Maldives has been renowned for its ambergris which comes from the gut of the sperm whale. This white, grey, or black substance is a great find for islanders since it fetches very high prices from the manufacturers of perfume and cosmetics. From time to time whale carcasses also get washed up on the reefs.

With such amazing coral reefs and great variety of marine life, it is not surprising that Maldives has become one of the great diving destinations in the world. On most resort islands there are well-run, well-equipped diving centres with excellent instructors who know their patch in Maldives like the backs of their hands.

It is, of course, possible to dive off any reef and to discover the stunning underwater world. During the last couple of decades, certain sites have become famous. The main ones are inevitably close to the resort islands around Malé, and carry names like Rainbow Reef, Paradise Rock, Paradise Pass, Blue Lagoon, Shallow Point, Potato Reef, Banana Reef, Coral Garden, and Fantasy Coral. Others are named after the fish you are likely to find there: Manta Point, Barracuda Giri, and Fusilier Reef. Shark Point and Lion's Head are well-known shark feeding sites.

On the outer wall of South Malé Atoll, stretching from Vaadhoo Island to Emboodhoo, there are several dramatic features on the reef edge, including a canyon, cathedral, and palisades. In the sandy bottom of Malé's outer harbour there is also the 100-metre-long wreck of the freighter *Maldive Victory*, which went down in February 1981 on Friday the thirteenth after hitting the south-west edge of Hulhule Island. Strong currents sweep across the hydroid-infested wreck that lies upright forty metres down.

In a typical dive off the 'house reef' of Vaadhoo Island, you would expect to see a couple of moray eels (willing to be stroked), lion and scorpion fish lying motionless on the coral (to be avoided), blue-barred jacks, groupers, and an assortment of surgeon, butterfly, and angelfish. In deep water, triggerfish flap along on their sides, while parrotfish excrete clouds of coral sand. Then a large dignified Napoleon wrasse might appear out of the blue.

The best way to reach the isolated 'wilderness' dives is to hire a *dhoani* and head off with an experienced skipper to the outer atolls.

Above: Colourful combination of hard and soft corals provides a welcome refuge for spotted sweetlips.

*Following pages: Beautiful disc-shaped coral spreading out to get maximum benefit from the sunlight. Such delicate forms can only grow inside the atoll basin where there are no fast currents or pounding waves. Taking advantage of these sheltered waters on the upper slope of the reef are orange butterfly perch (*Anthias squamipinnis*) which feed on zooplankton and do not grow more than eleven centimetres. The thin blue fish is a cleaner wrasse (*Labroides dimidiatus*) which picks parasites and dead skin from larger fish.*

There, lying at anchor off real desert islands, you can find coral reefs completely undisturbed by man.

To appreciate the full beauty of the corals and fish, it is always worth bearing in mind the effects of sunlight on water. Because of refraction objects seem closer and bigger than they really are. Colours change too. The deeper you go, the more light is filtered out by water.

Different colours are absorbed at different rates; within the first five metres all reds are filtered out, and red coral appears black. Orange appears black within ten metres, yellow will be completely absorbed by twenty metres, and green by twenty-five metres. The last to go is blue. Most objects appear blue or green. On any dive it makes sense to take a torch which will bring out the true colours.

Night diving with lights in these waters is unsurpassed for this is the time when all the corals open up and extend their polyps like so many flowers, and spiders and shrimps leave their tubular sponges to look for food. The moray eels are on the loose, as are the nocturnal predators like the batfish. Visibility, excellent by day, is reduced to the narrow tunnel of light from a torch. To bump into a shark out hunting by moonlight can be an unnerving experience indeed.

The maximum depth allowed for diving in Maldives is forty metres, but some resorts have wisely introduced their own limit of thirty metres. To go deeper, especially in the clear and warm water, is a constant temptation. It is easy to succumb to the excess of nitrogen in the blood — the notorious 'narcs' — which cause the often fatal 'raptures of the deep'.

The overwhelming sense of well-being and power can lead the most experienced diver to lose all caution and care. In such a state of euphoria divers have been known to offer the regulator of their air supply to passing fish. This feeling of elation is soon followed by confusion. Each year, experienced divers throughout the world disappear, drawn deeper and deeper over the blue edge, never to return.

It is easily understandable. Many lovers of the sea have experienced that 'oceanic feeling' of wanting to become absorbed by its pulsating immensity, to lose all sense of personal identity, to become part of the living whole.

One of the great diving attractions of Maldives used to be the shark feeds made famous by German photographer Herwath Voightmann on Bandos Island. The fashion caught on and at least five locations became popular — the house reef on Bandos, Lion's Head in the Vaadhoo Channel, Banana Reef near Furana, Rasfari near Nakatchafushi, and Fish Hole in Alifu Atoll.

Voightmann dressed up as an underwater superman and fed sharks mouth-to-mouth. Soon another more notorious human 'shark' turned up in the archipelago. Richard Harley was a lawyer who staged a diving accident in the Bahamas after being convicted of taking more than US$300,000 in bribes. Interpol at last caught up with him — yes, you guessed it, feeding sharks.

The feat is not as dangerous as it sounds. The knack is to feed them large fish, so that when one of them is in the shark's mouth, there is no more room for heads or hands. Since tuna send sharks crazy, it is better to use rainbow fish as bait.

It is still possible to see a shark feed, but it is becoming rarer for

several reasons. First, there is the danger to the feeders. Second, there is the damage done to the sharks themselves: touching a shark harms the protective covering on its body and makes it prone to infection.

Feeding also changes the sharks' natural behaviour, not only making them lazy feeders but training them to associate divers with food which can result in divers being molested. Then the shark-feeding sites themselves have become coral graveyards — underwater spectators sitting on the coral reef have killed them off.

With the growing ecological awareness among divers in recent years, shark-feeding causes the same negative overtones as a circus of wild animals. It is now widely recognized that man's impact on the marine environment should be kept to a minimum. It is better to observe the underwater world in Maldives as it is, without human interference, particularly as it is one of the last real 'wildernesses' left on earth. In keeping with this new spirit, the Maldivian government officially discourages the so-called 'shark circuses'.

The best way to appreciate the underwater world of Maldives is to go slowly, conserve energy, and look carefully around. Nothing compares to drifting along a reef edge, carried by the gentle current, the neutrally buoyant diver an honorary fish among fish, a harmless observer of the environment. There is so much unearthly beauty that afterwards many divers are unable to remember the exact details of all they have seen. They just recall a sense of deep contentment and peace.

Above: A golden belly anemone fish, also known as a clown fish, hovers within the tentacles of its host anemone.

People, of course, are land mammals and water is not our element. But if the evolutionists are right, all life began in the water and it is no surprise that so many feel at home once they have learned the basic rules of underwater survival. Many establish relationships with the fish; dolphins, of course, are famous for offering life-changing experiences, but even moray eels, with their doleful eyes, impart a certain knowledge and mutual empathy. Some diving instructors are emphatic that they have communicated with turtles in Maldivian waters.

For the present, the Indian Ocean is the least polluted sea in the world and Maldives does not suffer from major industrial pollution. But there are growing threats to its unique and fragile marine environment.

The most immediate problem comes from coral mining. Until this century, islanders used mainly *cadjan* for their homes, but it is now a status symbol to have a solid house and surrounding walls made from coral fragments. Throughout the archipelago, it is possible to see half-built coral houses while the owner is away earning more money in order to buy more coral to complete the job. The resort islands have copied this style for most of their buildings.

Since coral is taken from the top two metres of the reefs surrounding the islands it kills off the coral-building polyps. The result is that the islands are increasingly vulnerable to storms and tidal surges. Moreover, in 1986 cracks were observed in the reef around Malé.

Aware of the danger, the government is now encouraging the use of cement bricks, but this relies on expensive imported cement and local sand which is by no means limitless. As the population increases and tourism expands, the situation is likely to become worse.

Other human activities upset the natural equilibrium. The jetties and harbours on small islands prevent the natural circular movement of sand

*Following pages: Reef slope of wondrous corals provides shelter for the vermilion rock cod (*Cephalopholis miniata*). Of the same family as groupers, it lies motionless for long periods until an unwary fish or shrimp comes along and is suddenly snatched up and swallowed in one gulp. The competition between the soft and hard corals on this reef is intense; the fast-growing soft coral exuding toxic chemicals threatening to overtake the hard coral which fights back with stinging tentacles. The kaleidoscopic colours of the coral come from algae living within their polyps.*

around the islands according to the monsoons, resulting in erosion on one side and unwelcome silt on the other. The leaching of waste water on inhabited islands also encourages the growth of weeds around their shores.

The greatest hope lies in the growing ecological awareness of the Maldivian people who have begun to plant trees to consolidate the sand of their islands and to recognize that their life depends on the health of the coral reefs which protect them. While tourists have undoubtedly contributed to the degradation of the local environment in the past, they too are increasingly eager to preserve and protect the unique marine wilderness of Maldives.

But the problem is not only man-made. Coral forms an extremely delicate and carefully balanced ecosystem. Like all reefs, those in Maldives suffer from heavy rainfall which dilutes the salinity of the sea, from strong wave action, and from the exposure of reefs during exceptionally low tides. The result is extensive coral bleaching in some areas.

More recently, the reefs have also had to contend with an infestation of crown-of-thorns starfish, a large spiny creature which feeds on reef building corals and can reach plague proportions. In Maldives the first outbreaks were reported in Alifu Atoll in the mid-1970s. More recently, there has been an alarming outbreak north-west of Malé Atoll where, on some reefs, most reef-building coral has been killed.

Some scientists suggest that the sudden appearance of the crown-of-thorns is the result of human interference with the reef through coral mining and the removal of the crown-of-thorns' natural predator, the giant triton shell. Others stress that a sudden change in ocean conditions precipitates infestation. As yet there is little agreement on the long-term effects. Indeed, it has been argued that it is part of a natural cyclical process, only observed since diving became popular. It may well have a long-term benefit by removing fast-growing coral, thereby maintaining the diversity of the coral communities. Until that is proved, however, Malé Atoll is at least more vulnerable than before.

Human activity is beginning to affect other species of marine life. When the country first opened its doors to tourists, many divers plundered the reefs for shells but this has now been banned, along with spear fishing and the taking of any marine life from the waters surrounding the resort islands. It is still possible, however, to buy tortoiseshell jewellery (which has led to a serious decline in turtle numbers) as well as jewellery made from black coral (which has meant that this rare coral has virtually disappeared from the islands around Malé).

As far as fishing is concerned, only sea cucumbers and lobsters seem to be in decline because of excessive catches. It is tuna — the skipjack and yellow-fin variety — that Maldivians like to eat and export. At present tuna stocks seem to be holding up, despite increased catches due to mechanized boats and the use of freezer ships, mainly because Maldivian fishermen still use the traditional pole and line method to catch them.

Both species of tuna are migratory, however, travelling across the Indian Ocean from Seychelles to Sri Lanka. Although Maldives has an

Above: Flamboyant lionfish (Pterois volitans)*, a 'lie-in-wait' predator of the reef slope which grows up to thirty-five centimetres long and lives on small fish and crustaceans. In an attempt to warn off predators, it boldly displays the row of brightly coloured poisonous spines along its back.*

exclusive 330-kilometre zone around its islands, it cannot control the fishermen from Japan, Korea, and Taiwan who have been longlining in the region for tuna since the 1950s. More recently, French and Spanish purse seiners operating from Seychelles have been sweeping up schools of tuna. As stocks of tuna decline in the Atlantic, no doubt there will be increasing pressure on those in the Indian Ocean in the years to come.

The greatest long-term threat to Maldives, however, comes from something far more serious — global warming. It has now been firmly established by scientists that the greenhouse effect will lead to the melting of the ice caps and a rise in sea-level.

Scientists have predicted that within the next forty years sea-levels could rise between twenty-four and thirty-eight centimetres. Since nowhere in Maldives is higher than three metres this could be catastrophic. Not only do most islands form a cup-shape with a low centre, but some, like Malé, are actually sinking. All it needs is an increase of one metre in sea-level to make the islands extremely vulnerable to tidal surges and sudden storms.

Not all agree with this scenario. Optimists point out that fast-growing,

Overleaf: Tourist enjoys sundowner cocktail as the Indian Ocean turns to gold.

'catch-up' coral reefs can grow ten centimetres a year and should be able to keep pace with the expected rise in sea-level. Unfortunately, most of the protective reefs around the islands grow slowly — the slowest rises one centimetre every ten years. Moreover, fast corals grow where the current is weakest and the threat the least.

Others argue that nature knows best and somehow will take care of itself. There can be no doubt that a coral reef has a remarkable capacity to heal itself; any diver who has seen coral growing over a bottle can confirm this.

The reef is a living organism and the whole is greater than its parts. But with the present level of human interference there is little room for nature to work its healing ways.

Even if enough coral keeps pace with the rise in sea-level, just as worrying are the climatic changes associated with global warming. The aberrant weather pattern known as El Niño, previously thought to be confined only to the southern Pacific, now seems to affect the Indian Ocean. There have been many more storms in the area recently.

One day soon, perhaps during an exceptionally high tide, storm-driven waves may well sweep across the islands, washing all the hard-won vegetation, neat houses, beautifully carved tombstones, and ancient ruins over the edge of the reefs.

All that would be left would be some sand spits and coral debris, and perhaps some intriguing sites for divers searching for traces of a lost civilization. In time, Maldivians might be transplanted to higher ground on the mainland of Asia, but their unique language, culture, and way of life would soon disappear forever.

Unless they change their way of life at home, the tourists who flock to Maldives today to enjoy a touch of unspoilt 'tropical paradise' will be directly responsible for its demise.

The poet John Donne once wrote 'no man is an island, entire of itself'; in our fragile and polluted world, no island, however small, remains self-contained. And if the Maldive islands were to disappear, we would all be the losers.